D0270075

DEVELOPMENT

IN   PRACTICE

A New Agenda for Women's Health and Nutrition

A New Agenda
for Women's Health
and Nutrition

THE WORLD BANK
WASHINGTON, D.C.

The Development in Practice series publishes reviews of the World Bank's
activities in different regions and sectors. It lays particular emphasis on the
progress that is being made and on the policies and practices that hold the most
promise of success in the effort to reduce poverty in the developing world.

This report is a study by the World Bank's staff, and the judgments made herein
do not necessarily reflect the views of the Board of Executive Directors or of the
governments they represent.

Cover photographs: *(top left)* World Bank/Burkina Faso/Curt Carnemark;
(top middle) UNICEF/Yemen C-99(2)/N. Toutounji; *(top right)* World Bank/Nepal/
Curt Carnemark; *(bottom left)* World Bank/Guatemala/Curt Carnemark; *(bottom
right)* World Bank/China/Curt Carnemark.

Library of Congress Cataloging-in-Publication Data

A New agenda for women's health and nutrition.
     p.   cm. —   (Development in practice)
  Includes bibliographical references (p. 87).
  ISBN 0-8213-3009-8
    1. Women—Health and hygiene—Developing countries. 2. Women—
Developing countries—Nutrition. 3. Women's health services—
Developing countries. I. International Bank for Reconstruction
and Development. II. Series: Development in practice (Washington,
D.C.).
RA564.85.N48   1994
362.1'082—dc20
                             94-29586
                              CIP

Contents

TABLES

Acknowledgments

This report was prepared by a team led by Anne Tinker and composed of Patricia Daly, Cynthia Green, Helen Saxenian, Rama Lakshminarayanan, and Kirrin Gill. The team benefited from contributions and advice from a large number of people, both within and outside the World Bank. Diana Measham provided assistance in condensing a lengthier version of this report (Tinker and others 1994) into this document. Throughout the planning and preparation, an external peer review committee consisting of Mahmoud Fathalla, Judith Fortney, John Kevany, Ana Langer, and Joanne Leslie provided technical review and invaluable guidance.

This report and the longer paper on which it is based grew out of ten working papers commissioned by the Bank. These working papers explored critical topics in women's health and nutrition, from the socioeconomic factors that influence women's access to nutrition and health care to the subjects of adolescent health and violence against women. The authors of those papers include George Ascadi, Gwendolyn Johnson-Ascadi, Jill Gay, Lori Heise, Joe Kutzin, Kathleen Merchant, May Post, Judith Senderowitz, Jacqueline Sherris, Kajsa Sundström, and Mary Eming Young. The report also draws on a recent World Bank Discussion Paper, *Making Motherhood Safe* (Tinker and Koblinsky 1993), as well as on the disease burden assessment and cost-effectiveness analysis prepared for *World Development Report 1993: Investing in Health* (World Bank 1993b).

Financial support for this document was provided by the World Bank, the Swedish International Development Authority, the Swiss Development Cooperation, and the Overseas Development Administration of the United Kingdom.

Acronyms and Data Note

AIDS	Acquired immunodeficiency syndrome
DALY	Disability-adjusted life year
HIV	Human immunodeficiency virus
IUD	Intrauterine device
NGO	Nongovernmental organization
RTI	Reproductive tract infection
SIDA	Swedish International Development Authority
STD	Sexually transmitted disease
TBA	Traditional birth attendant
UNDP	United Nations Development Programme
UNFPA	United Nations Population Fund
UNICEF	United Nations Children's Fund
WHO	World Health Organization

Note: All dollar amounts ($) are current U.S. dollars.

Executive Summary

Investment in women's health and nutrition promotes equity, widespread benefits for this generation and the next, and economic efficiency. Women's disproportionate poverty, low social status, and reproductive role expose them to high health risks, resulting in needless and largely preventable suffering and death. A woman's health and nutritional status is a national as well as an individual welfare concern because it also affects the next generation, through its impact on her children and her economic productivity. Because many of the interventions that address women's health problems are highly cost-effective, any national investment strategy based on achieving the greatest health gains at the least cost will give considerable emphasis to health interventions directed at women. Special attention is warranted to reach women during adolescence, when reproductive and other lifestyle behaviors set the stage for later life.

Women's Health throughout the Life Cycle

A life-cycle approach to women's health takes into account both the specific and the cumulative effects of poor health and nutrition. Many of the health problems that affect women of reproductive age, their newborns, and older women begin in childhood and adolescence. For example, inadequate diet in youth and adolescence can lead to anemia or stunting, which contribute to complications in childbirth and underweight babies, and insufficient calcium can lead to osteoporosis later in life. The following examples provide a brief sketch of some of the health and nutrition problems women face in developing countries.

■ In Africa each year, an estimated 2 million young girls are subject to genital mutilation (removal of parts or all of the external female genitals).

■ In many countries of South Asia, Africa, Latin America, and the Middle East, one-third to one-half of women are mothers before the age of 20. In a few countries, as many as one in four girls is married before her fifteenth birthday.

■ Women are at greater risk than men of contracting the human immunodeficiency virus (HIV) when exposed to an infected partner, and young girls are the most vulnerable. Of all women infected, 70 percent are between the ages of 15 and 25.

■ Anemia is highly prevalent throughout the developing world and appears to be worsening in South Asia, for example, where it affects at least 60 percent of all women aged 15–49.

■ Worldwide, one in four pregnancies is unwanted. Abortions outnumer live births in parts of Eastern Europe and the former Soviet Union. Complications from unsafe abortion are a major cause of maternal death.

■ While infant mortality rates have fallen by one-half in the past thirty years, maternal mortality ratios have lagged behind, with little evidence of progress in the least developed countries.

■ Cancer of the cervix, which peaks in women aged 40–50, accounts for more new cases of cancer each year in developing countries than any other type of cancer.

■ Domestic violence, rape, and sexual abuse are a significant cause of disability among women.

Essential Services for Women

Most of the leading causes of death and disability among women in developing countries can be prevented or treated through highly cost-effective interventions. Any national package of interventions designed on the basis of cost-effectiveness and the disease burden would include the following essential services for women:

- Prevention and management of unwanted pregnancies.
- Safe pregnancy and delivery services.
- Prevention and management of sexually transmitted diseases.
- Promotion of positive health practices, such as safe sex and adequate nutrition.
- Prevention of practices harmful to health, such as less food and health care for girls than boys and violence against women.

In even the poorest countries, governments can help to establish and ensure access to these essential services by financing the health interventions for the poor and the behavioral change interventions for the entire population. Services beyond the national package should be financed from private sources. Where resources permit a more comprehensive national package of interventions, the essential services could be expanded and upgraded to include:

- A wider choice of short- and long-term contraceptive methods.
- Enhanced maternity care.
- Expanded screening for and treatment of sexually transmitted diseases.
- Nutrition assistance for vulnerable groups.
- Cervical and breast cancer screening and treatment.
- Increased attention to early prevention of disease.
- Increased policy dialogue and strategic efforts to reduce gender discrimination and violence.
- Greater attention to the health problems of women beyond reproductive age.

What Actions Are Needed

Governments can improve women's health by enacting and promoting gender-sensitive policies and strengthening women's health services. Efforts to redress socioeconomic inequities must complement health sector reform. Existing services can be improved, extended, and tailored to fit local conditions. For example, where cultural norms discourage women from receiving care from men, governments could recruit and train more female health providers. Collection and analysis of gender-specific information on health care utilization and health status can guide these efforts. Finally, education can promote positive health behaviors and change harmful attitudes and conduct.

By working closely with the private sector to deliver information and services, governments can help derive the greatest benefits from national health resources. Nongovernmental organizations that are well respected in the community can be helpful in reaching and representing disadvantaged women. Private, for-profit providers can supplement government programs by offering a broader range of services to those who can afford to pay for them.

By increasing policymakers' awareness of the real social and economic gains emanating from improvements in women's health, foreign assistance agencies—including the World Bank—can have an impact far beyond their monetary contribution. International agencies can help by informing country decisionmakers about lessons gleaned from worldwide experience and by supporting interventions proven to be cost-effective. External inputs may be particularly helpful in the design of demonstration projects and the expansion of women's health programs to the national scale.

■ ■ ■

A New Agenda for Women's Health and Nutrition focuses on actions that can be taken by the health sector, although it also argues for broader efforts (in female education and employment, for example). Its recommendations are based on concerns for human welfare and economic efficiency. The paper suggests essential clinical and public health interventions, discusses factors to be considered in program planning and implementation, and describes ways that assistance agencies can facilitate programs.

Chapter 1 presents the rationale for financing interventions to improve women's health and nutrition. Chapter 2 summarizes the health problems affecting women. Chapter 3 describes the essential and expanded health services recommended for women in low- and middle-income countries. Chapter 4 discusses key aspects of planning and implementing a national women's health program, including the impact of government policies, the need for government financing, collaboration with the private sector, the quality of care, and data requirements. Chapter 5 outlines ways that international assistance agencies can contribute to improvements in women's health services through policy dialogue, sector work, project preparation, funding for research, and donor coordination. It also discusses women's health problems and potential strategies on a regional basis.

This document is based on another publication, *Women's Health and Nutrition: Making a Difference* (Tinker and others 1994), which was developed by World Bank staff and colleagues from around the world to assist in the design and implementation of women's health and nutrition programs. Readers interested in more information are encouraged to consult that publication and its annexes, which contain greater detail on women's health and nutrition problems, recommended interventions by level of health care, and indicators of women's health and nutrition.

CHAPTER ONE

Why Invest in Women's Health and Nutrition?

Evidence from around the world has demonstrated that investment in health is fundamental to improving human welfare and economic growth, as well as to reducing poverty (World Bank 1993b). This report focuses on how public investment in women's health and nutrition, in particular, can contribute to sustainable economic growth by:

■ *Improving equity and the quality of life.* Initiatives to improve women's health could save millions of women from needless suffering or premature death and enable them to lead fully productive lives. Women are at particularly high risk for certain health problems, largely because of their low socioeconomic status and reproductive role.

■ *Conferring widespread benefits.* Investments in women's health have multiple payoffs. In addition to improving women's well-being and productivity, such investments also yield significant benefits for families, communities, and the national economy. In particular, women's health has a major impact on the health and productivity of the next generation.

■ *Improving efficiency.* Redirecting public spending to highly cost-effective interventions improves allocative efficiency. Measures that address women's health problems are among the most cost-effective investments available in developing countries.

1

Differentials in Health

Fertility and infant and child mortality rates have dropped substantially in developing countries over the past three decades. From 1962 to 1992, infant mortality in the developing world decreased by 50 percent, and fertility rates fell by 40 percent (UN 1993). Fertility regulation has contributed to women's health by reducing the number of pregnancies—and the associated risks—and giving women more control over their lives.

Progress has been much slower in other areas significant to women's health. Maternal mortality ratios and rates reflect the widest disparity in human development indicators between industrial and developing countries.[1] In Sub-Saharan Africa, for example, where the ratio is 700 maternal deaths per 100,000 live births, a woman runs a 1 in 22 risk of dying from pregnancy-related causes during her lifetime. In Northern Europe, the risk falls to 1 in 10,000 (UN 1993; Herz and Measham 1987). Except in countries with relatively low maternal mortality ratios (fewer than 100 maternal deaths per 100,000 births), the World Health Organization (WHO) has found scant evidence of any progress in reducing maternal mortality in recent years (WHO 1992c). In Bangladesh, for example, although the total fertility rate declined by one-third and child mortality by almost one-half in just over two decades, the maternal mortality ratio remained virtually unchanged (Khan, Jahan, and Begum 1986; World Bank 1992; World Bank 1993a).

As it now stands, most women in the developing world lack ready access to a selection of fertility control methods and to basic maternity care. Many countries have largely neglected interventions that could control other problems to which women are particularly vulnerable, such as sexually transmitted diseases (STDs), malnutrition, and gender violence. Moreover, the women's health initiatives that are in place are inadequate and tend to focus on married women of childbearing age. Girls, adolescents, older women, and unmarried or childless women of reproductive age rarely receive the attention of public health administrators.

Women's health status is affected by complex biological, social, and cultural factors that are highly interrelated (Figure 1.1). To reach women effectively, health systems must take into account the biological factors that increase health risks for women and such sociocultural determinants of health as age at marriage, as well as psychological factors, such as depression arising from gender violence. Over the longer term, broader efforts—particularly increased female education—will help reduce many of the barriers to women's health.

---

1. The maternal mortality ratio is the number of women who die in pregnancy and childbirth per 100,000 live births. It measures the risk women face of dying once pregnant. The maternal mortality rate is the number of women dying in pregnancy or childbirth per 100,000 women aged 15–49. The rate reflects both the maternal mortality ratio and the fertility rate.

FIGURE 1.1 DETERMINANTS OF WOMEN'S HEALTH STATUS

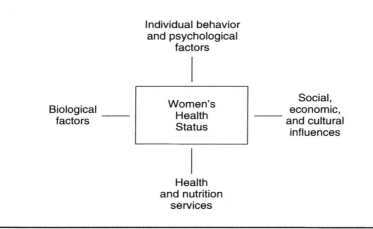

Biological Determinants of Women's Health

Under optimal conditions for both men and women, a woman's life expectancy at birth is 1.03 times that of men (Coale and Demeny 1983; World Bank 1993b). In many parts of the world the statistics are even more favorable for females; in most industrial countries their life expectancy is more than 1.06 times that of men, and up to 1.10 times higher in Canada. In most developing countries, however, the ratio is much lower, dropping below 1.00 in parts of Asia with a low of 0.97 in Bhutan—a sign of socioeconomic conditions particularly inimical to women and girls (Keyfitz and Flieger 1990).

While the major health risks related to pregnancy are well known, other health problems associated with women's reproductive biology may be less recognized. Menstruation, for example, renders women more susceptible than men to iron-deficiency anemia. Certain conditions, including anemia, malaria, and tuberculosis, can be exacerbated by pregnancy. Complications of pregnancy may also cause permanent damage, such as uterine prolapse and obstetric fistulae.

Because of biological factors, women have a higher risk per exposure of contracting STDs, including HIV, than do men. In addition, because women with STDs are more likely to have no symptoms, they may delay treatment until an advanced stage, with more severe consequences. Human papillomavirus infection results in genital cancer much more frequently in women than in men, and it is the single most important risk factor for cancer of the cervix, which accounts for more new cases of cancer each year in developing countries than any other type of cancer (Parkin, Laara, and Muir 1988). And although women of reproductive age are thought to receive some protection against cardiovascular disease from the hormone estrogen, their risk increases after menopause. By age 65, a higher proportion of women than men die as a consequence of cardiovascular conditions (Lopez 1993).

Although the reasons are not well understood, women tend to have fewer injuries than men. The behavior patterns of men, including higher alcohol consumption, place them at a higher risk for most injuries, but biology may also play a role (Stansfield, Smith, and McGreevey 1993).

Socioeconomic Influences on Women's Health

The cultural and socioeconomic environment affects women's exposure to disease and injury, their diet, their access to and use of health services, and the manifestations and consequences of disease. Indoor cooking, for example, is one of the most serious occupational health and environmental hazards in the developing world because of the acute and chronic—and sometimes fatal—consequences of inhalation of smoke and toxic gases, as well as accidental burnings (WHO 1986; World Bank 1992).

Women's disadvantaged social position, which is often related to the economic value placed on familial roles, helps perpetuate poor health, inadequate diet, early and frequent pregnancy, and a continued cycle of poverty. From infancy, females in many parts of the world receive less and lower-quality food and are treated less often when sick, and then only at a more advanced stage of disease. In countries where women are less educated, receive less information than men, and have less control over decisionmaking and family resources, they are also less apt to recognize health problems or to seek care. Cultural factors, such as restrictions in some Middle Eastern countries on women's traveling alone or being treated by male health care providers, inhibit their use of health services.

Women's low socioeconomic status can also expose them to physical and sexual abuse and mental depression. Unequal power in sexual relationships exposes women to unwanted pregnancy and STDs, including HIV and acquired immunodeficiency syndrome (AIDS). With changing social values and economic pressures, girls are engaging in sexual relationships at earlier ages. The worst manifestation of this phenomenon is the growing number of young girls forced into prostitution, especially in Asia.

The general level of underdevelopment may pose additional health risks for women. For example, poor roads and lack of transport, as well as inadequate obstetric facilities, hinder women from receiving timely medical treatment for pregnancy-related complications. Inadequate water supply, lack of electricity, and poor sanitation impose extra burdens on women because of their household responsibilities, such as fetching water and fuelwood.

Women's disproportionate poverty further curtails their access to health services. Their wages for the same or similar work are substantially lower than men's, and much of their work is outside the formal sector and not financially remunerated. Furthermore, because of their multiple tasks and responsibilities, women face high opportunity costs for time spent on health care. Girls begin working at an earlier age than boys and spend more hours working each day (paid and unpaid) throughout their lives in all regions (UN 1991). Studies in Kenya and Peru confirm that distance and user fees are a larger obstacle to women than to men in seeking medical care (Mwabu, Ainsworth, and Nyamete 1993; Gertler and van der Gaag 1990).

The strongest evidence of gender differentials in health status and the use of health services has been documented for both children and adults in South Asia. A study in India found that protein-energy malnutrition was four to five times more prevalent among girls, and yet boys were fifty times more likely to be hospitalized for treatment (Das Gupta 1987). Studies in other countries have also found that even where there is no apparent gender difference in the prevalence of infectious disease, women may be less likely than men to seek care. In Colombia and Thailand, for example, about six times as many adult men as women attend malaria clinics for treatment (Vlassof and Bonilla 1992; Ettling and others 1989).

The Widespread Impact of Women's Health

Improving women's health has significant benefits not only for women but also for their children and the national economy. Standard cost-effectiveness calculations often fail to take these effects into account.

Child Survival and Family Welfare

To a large extent, the well-being of children depends on the health of their mothers. In developing countries, a mother's death in childbirth means almost certain death for the newborn and severe consequences for her older children. A recent study in Bangladesh of children up to age 10 found that a mother's death sharply increases the chances that her children, especially her daughters, will die within two years. Children whose mothers die are three to ten times more likely to die within two years than those with living parents (Figure 1.2). A father's death only has a significant effect on the survival prospects of his children between the ages of 5 and 9, and the impact is just half that of the mother's death (Strong 1992).

When mothers are malnourished, sickly, or receive inadequate care in pregnancy, their children face a higher risk of disease and death. The effect on perinatal outcomes is particularly strong. Each year, 7 million infants die

FIGURE 1.2 RELATION BETWEEN CHILD'S PROBABILITY OF DYING AND MOTHER'S DEATH, MATLAB, BANGLADESH, 1983–89

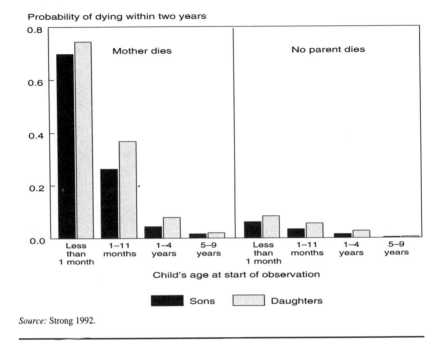

Probability of dying within two years

Source: Strong 1992.

within a week of birth and more than 20 million low-birthweight babies are born. The prospects for many of these babies could be bettered by improving women's health and nutrition and providing good maternity care (WHO 1993a; WHO and UNICEF 1992).

Maternal anemia and small pelvic size among women whose growth has been stunted increase the risk of infant mortality. Iodine-deficient mothers are at greater risk of giving birth to infants with severe mental retardation and other congenital abnormalities. Pregnancy in early adolescence has additional harmful effects and sets in motion an intergenerational cycle of ill health and growth failure. Proper nutrition and health care can interrupt this cycle.

A woman's health status affects not only her children's health but also other aspects of their welfare. The preliminary results of a study in Tanzania suggest that a woman's death has an important influence on children's education, particularly at the secondary school level. In households where an adult woman had died within the past twelve months, children spent only one-half as much time in school as did children from households where such a death had not occurred. The effect did not appear significant when an adult male died (Ainsworth and Over 1994).

As the principal providers of family health care, women tend to the sick and disabled and protect children's health. Although not officially recognized as health workers, women are responsible for 70 to 80 percent of all the health care provided in developing countries. Therefore, improving their health status and educating them to prevent and detect infectious diseases and practice proper hygiene and nutrition is a cost-effective approach to improving family health (Leslie, Lycette, and Buvinic 1988).

Productivity and Poverty Reduction

Reducing fertility and improving women's health can improve individual productivity and family well-being and, particularly when combined with education and access to jobs, can also accelerate a nation's economic development. Women's current contributions are substantial but only partially reflected in official economic statistics, and women's potential is underutilized. Women are responsible for up to three-quarters of the food produced annually in the developing world. In parts of Africa, women produce 80 percent of the food consumed domestically and at least 50 percent of export crops. Women also constitute one-third of the world's wage-labor force and one-fourth of the industrial labor force. Much of women's work—both within and outside the home—is unpaid and therefore not counted. If the gross domestic product (GDP) included domestic work, it would increase by 25 percent (UN 1991).

Poor health reduces women's capacity to carry out their multiple productive and reproductive responsibilities. Studies of women tea workers in Sri Lanka and cotton mill workers in China, for example, have documented the reduced productivity associated with iron deficiency and the positive effects of iron supplementation on work output (Edgerton and others 1979; Li and others 1994). Frequent pregnancies and poor health not only drain women's productive energy but also contribute to their poverty. A study in one area of India found that disability reduced the female labor force by 22 percent. In addition, illness was found to be the second highest cause of indebtedness—with especially profound effects on women because they predominate among the poor (Chatterjee 1991).

Women's health is central not only to their wage earning but also to the performance of their many household tasks. Within the family, women bear the principal responsibility for maintaining the home and caring for society's dependents—children and the elderly. They collect water and fuel (Tanzanian women, for example, use up to 20 percent of their caloric intake collecting water), they cook and feed the family, and they perform other tasks essential to household maintenance. These familial responsibilities carry high opportunity costs, as reflected in absenteeism from the work force associated with pregnancy or the care of sick children, for example.

Evidence suggests that efforts to improve the health and nutritional status of women could be critical to the goal of poverty reduction. The weight of poverty falls more heavily on women than on men. In addition to low health and nutritional status, poor women have low education levels. In the developing world there are only 86 females per 100 males in primary school, 75 in secondary school, and 64 in tertiary education. Finally, women have less access to remunerative activities.

Female-headed households are becoming more prevalent and already represent 20 percent of all households in Africa and in Latin America and the Caribbean (UN 1991). Among the poor, female-headed households are at a greater economic disadvantage than male- or jointly headed households because of the lower earnings of women and the dual nature of their work burden, which imposes severe time constraints, restricting their access to social and health services (Rosenhouse 1989).

Despite these disadvantages, women contribute a large share of household income for family survival. Evidence from diverse country settings—Burkina Faso, Cameroon, India, Lebanon, Nepal, and the Philippines—suggests that when the time spent on home production is valued, women contribute between 40 to 60 percent of household income (World Bank 1994). Women are also more likely than men to spend their income on family welfare. In Guatemala it takes fifteen times more spending to achieve a given improvement in child nutrition when income is earned by the father than when it is earned by the mother (World Bank 1993b).

Investing in women is a major theme of the World Bank's two-pronged strategy for poverty reduction, which includes (a) the introduction of broadly based, labor-absorbing economic growth to generate income-earning opportunities for the poor and (b) improved access to education, health care, and other social services to help the poor take advantage of these opportunities (World Bank 1994). The adverse effects of ill health, both on income and on personal and household welfare, are greatest for the poor. There is evidence that improved health and nutrition reduces infant and child mortality and contributes to demand for smaller families. Smaller family size in turn helps reduce poverty by saving household resources. A growing body of research also points to the positive effects of health and nutrition on the labor productivity of the poor (Behrman 1990). Therefore, to the extent that women are overrepresented among the poor, interventions for improving women's health and nutrition are critical to efforts for poverty reduction.

The Cost-Effectiveness of Women's Health Interventions

An analysis of the eighteen most cost-effective interventions that affect the leading causes of death and disability for both sexes found that childhood interventions have similar benefits for males and females. Men benefit more than women from the treatment of tuberculosis after age 15 and from prevention of conditions related to tobacco and alcohol consumption after age 45. From age 5 onward, however, females benefit more than males from the prevention and treatment of STDs and iron-deficiency anemia. In addition, women derive substantial benefits from interventions that target health problems exclusive to women, such as cervical cancer.

For the major causes of death and disability for males and females by age group in developing countries, there is a greater convergence of the relative disease burden and cost-effective interventions for females than for males (Table 1.1). Highly cost-effective interventions—those costing less than $100 per disability-adjusted life year (DALY) saved—can benefit more females than males between the ages of 5 and 44. The health problems of women aged 15 to 44—especially those related to reproduction—are particularly responsive to cost-effective prevention and treatment. For these reasons, many of the interventions included in the minimum package of health services considered essential by the World Bank (Box 1.1) either directly benefit girls and women or are targeted to them as a means of improving infant health. In low-income countries, for example, one-third of the cost of the recommended minimum

TABLE 1.1 MAJOR HEALTH PROBLEMS WITH INTERVENTIONS OF HIGH TO MEDIUM COST-EFFECTIVENESS, IN DEVELOPING COUNTRIES, 1990

	Cost-effectiveness of intervention			
Age group/ main causes of disease	Diseases affecting females only	Diseases greater among females[a]	Diseases similar among males and females[b]	Diseases greater among males[c]
Ages 0–4				
Respiratory infections	—	—	High	—
Perinatal causes	—	—	High	—
Diarrheal disease	—	—	High	—
Childhood cluster[d]	—	—	High	—
Malaria	—	—	High	—
Protein-energy malnutrition	—	—	High	—
Vitamin A deficiency	—	—	High	—
Iodine deficiency	—	—	High	—
STDs and HIV	—	—	High	—
Ages 5–14				
Intestinal helminths	—	—	High	—
Childhood cluster[d]	—	—	High	—

(Table continues on the following page.)

TABLE 1.1 (*continued*)

	Cost-effectiveness of intervention			
Age group/ main causes of disease	Diseases affecting females only	Diseases greater among females[a]	Diseases similar among males and females[b]	Diseases greater among males[c]
Ages 5–14 (*continued*)				
Respiratory infections	—	—	High	—
Diarrheal disease	—	—	High	—
Tuberculosis	—	High	—	—
Malaria	—	—	High	—
Anemias	—	High	—	—
STDs and HIV	—	High	—	—
Ages 15–44				
Maternal causes	High	—	—	—
STDS	—	High	—	—
Tuberculosis	—	—	High	—
HIV	—	—	—	High
Depressive disorders	—	Medium	—	—
Respiratory infections	—	—	High	—
Anemia	—	High	—	—
Ages 45–59				
Tuberculosis	—	—	—	High
Ischemic heart disease	—	—	—	Medium
Cataracts	—	High	—	—
Chronic obstructive pulmonary diseases	—	—	Medium	—
Diabetes mellitus	—	Medium	—	—
Cancer of the cervix	High	—	—	—
Malignant neoplasm (liver)	—	—	—	High
Ages 60+				
Ischemic heart disease	—	—	Medium	—
Respiratory infections	—	—	High	—
Diabetes mellitus	—	Medium	—	—
Tuberculosis	—	—	—	High
Cataracts	—	—	High	—
Malignant neoplasms (trachea, bronchus, lung)	—	—	—	High

Note: The causes of disease shown here have been chosen from the ten main causes among women and the ten main causes among men based on the availability of an intervention of high or medium cost-effectiveness. Interventions of high cost-effectiveness are those that can be implemented for less than $100 per disability-adjusted life year (DALY) saved; those of medium cost-effectiveness, for $100–999 per DALY saved.
a. For which the ratio of female to male burden of disease is 0.8 or less.
b. For which the ratio of female to male burden of disease is between 0.8 and 1.2.
c. For which the ratio of male to female burden of disease is 0.8 or less.
d. Vaccine-preventable diseases of childhood.
Source: World Bank 1993b.

BOX 1.1 ASSESSING THE DISEASE
BURDEN AND INVESTING IN
INTERVENTIONS

Assessments of the relative importance of different health problems are
usually based on how many deaths
they cause. Many health problems,
however, are not fatal but cause much
disability. As part of background work
for the the 1993 edition of its annual
World Development Report, the World
Bank, in collaboration with WHO, car-
ried out a comprehensive analysis of
the disease burden—the amount of
both premature death and disability
due to specific diseases and injuries,
measured in disability-adjusted life
years (DALYs).

The burden of disease was calcu-
lated as the present value of future
DALYs lost as a result of death, disease, or injury in 1990. The calculations incorporated disability weights
(to value the severity of an illness relative to loss of life), discounting (to
value future years of healthy life relative to the present), and age weights
(to give years lost at different ages
different relative values). Using this
method, the disease burden was as-
sessed for more than 100 causes of
ill health, and the data broken down
by age, sex, and region. Preliminary
results appear in World Development
Report 1993 (World Bank 1993b). A
full accounting will be published jointly
by WHO and the World Bank.

Disease burden estimates can be
used to monitor global and country-
level progress in improving health,
and, in combination with information
on cost-effectiveness, to help set priorities for the health sector. Following
this approach, the World Bank as-

sessed the costs and benefits of a
wide range of health interventions to
determine which were the most cost-
effective. It then proposed a minimum
package of essential health services
that included:

■ Public health services—immunization, school health, AIDS prevention,
tobacco and alcohol control, and other
public health programs (including family planning, health and nutrition information).
■ Clinical services—short-course
chemotherapy for tuberculosis, management of the sick child, prenatal
and delivery care, family planning,
treatment of STDs, and limited care
for adults.

Where instituted, this minimum
package, which is estimated to cost
$12 per capita in low-income coun-
tries and $22 per capita in middle-
income countries, could reduce the
burden of disease in low-income countries by more than 30 percent and
about 15 percent in middle-income
countries. Public financing is needed
to ensure the availability of public
health interventions, given that such
services are so nearly public goods
that private markets will provide too
little of them. Governments must also
finance clinical services in the minimum package for the poor. In middle-
income countries, where resources
are less constrained, additional public expenditure can go either toward
extending coverage to the nonpoor or
toward expansion beyond the minimum package to a national package
of health care that includes somewhat
less cost-effective interventions for
more diseases and conditions.

package is accounted for by family planning, maternity care, and management of STDs; in middle-income countries these interventions account for half of the estimated costs (World Bank 1993b).

In sum, improvements in women's health increase personal and family well-being and productivity today and help to ensure healthier generations tomorrow. National economies, communities, and households—all of them highly dependent on women's paid and unpaid labor—benefit from investment in women's health.

CHAPTER TWO

An Overview of Women's Health and Nutrition

W omen's health status varies widely both within and among countries because of such factors as local disease prevalence, health-related behaviors, and women's educational attainment, exposure to health information, influence on decisionmaking, and access to health care. Poverty, environmental degradation, civil conflict, and migration also influence women's health.

Global Trends

In the developing world, women's health status is changing in response to several emerging trends.

■ *More education*. Girls who have attended school, especially through the secondary level, are more likely to delay marriage and childbearing, have smaller families, and use health care facilities (Schultz 1989).

■ *Later marriage*. In most countries women are marrying later, which generally implies postponed childbearing and permits women to stay in school longer. It also implies that growing numbers of adolescent girls are exposed to the risks associated with premarital sexual intercourse, such as unwanted pregnancy and STDs, including HIV.

■ *Emergence of HIV/AIDS.* The rate of HIV/AIDS infection is accelerating more rapidly among women than men, through exposure to infected partners. Young women are at particular risk.

■ *Smaller families.* Women are bearing children over increasingly short periods of their lives. For the average woman in developing countries with relatively low fertility rates, such as Indonesia and Mexico, fifteen years elapse between the first and last birth—less than 20 percent of the mother's lifetime. In countries with higher fertility and lower life expectancy, such as Kenya and Senegal, the average interval is nineteen to twenty years, or about 40 percent of a woman's lifetime. Comparable intervals are eight years for women in the United States and two years for those in Japan (Freedman and Blanc 1991).

■ *Longer life expectancy.* Life expectancy at birth has increased, primarily because of improved survival of infants and young children. As a result, health problems that emerge later in life, such as cervical cancer and cardiovascular disease, are becoming more prevalent, shifting health care concerns to those associated with chronic diseases, for which interventions tend to be less effective and more costly. Women constitute a majority of the elderly.

■ *Increased labor force participation.* Women are entering the formal labor force in growing numbers. Along with the positive benefits of increased income and, in some settings, social support, women face new occupational health hazards and the challenge of coordinating employment outside the home with such traditional responsibilities as breastfeeding and childcare.

Women's Burden of Disease

Because women live longer than men, the common belief is that they are healthier. In reality, women are more likely to experience poor health. A recent study that compared measures of ill health in several countries concluded that even though women live longer, they are more sickly and disabled than men throughout the life cycle (Strauss and others 1992).

Data from *World Development Report 1993* (World Bank 1993b) indicate that between the ages of 15 and 44 and after age 60, men generally have higher rates of premature death and women have higher rates of disability. Female disability is especially high in Asia, Sub-Saharan Africa, and the Middle East, and much of it is attributable to maternal causes, STDs, and gender-based discrimination.

In developing countries, one-third of the DALYs lost by women aged 15 to 44 result from reproductive health problems, with gender violence and rape accounting for an additional 5 percent (World Bank 1993b). More than one-fifth of the DALYs lost by women aged 45 to 59 can be attributed to conditions that exclusively or predominantly affect women. Although the potential gains from health interventions targeting women over 45 are more modest than those applied in earlier years, certain interventions, such as screening and cryotherapy for preinvasive cervical cancer, are highly effective and relatively cheap.

Women's Health and Nutrition throughout Life

Biological and social factors affect women's health throughout their lives and have cumulative effects. It is therefore important to consider the entire life cycle when examining the causes and consequences of women's poor health. For example, girls who are fed inadequately during childhood may have stunted growth, leading to higher risks of complications during childbirth. Similarly, sexual abuse or female genital mutilation during childhood increase the likelihood of poor physical and mental health in later years. Although the adolescent period overlaps with the reproductive years, it is considered separately here because of the long-term consequences of health problems during this period (Figure 2.1).

Different health and nutrition problems affect females at different stages of the life cycle, from infancy and childhood to adolescence and the reproductive years to the postreproductive period. For developing countries as a whole, 25 percent of females are aged 0 to 9, 21 percent are 10 to 19, 36 percent are 20 to 45, and 18 percent are over 45.

Infancy and Childhood

Girls are born with certain inherent biological advantages that make them less vulnerable than boys to childhood diseases, given equal nutrition, health conditions, and health care. However, discrimination in the treatment of girls can negate their innate biological advantages. In many developing countries girls are in poorer health than boys because of inadequate nutrition and health care. Such disparities are greatest in India and China, where more girls than boys die before their fifth birthday (World Bank 1993b). In a number of other developing countries with recent national surveys, girls are also more likely to die than boys (Figure 2.2). The key factors that adversely affect girls' health include the following.

Discriminatory childcare. In societies where boys are more highly valued than girls, boys may receive more preventive care and more timely attention when they fall ill. In some societies girls receive less food and less nutritious food than boys (Ravindran 1986), leading to malnutrition and impaired physical development.

FIGURE 2.1 HEALTH AND NUTRITION PROBLEMS AFFECTING WOMEN EXCLUSIVELY
OR PREDOMINANTLY DURING THE LIFE CYCLE

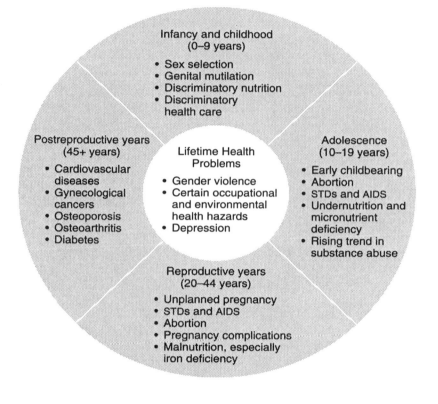

Infancy and childhood
(0–9 years)

• Sex selection
• Genital mutilation
• Discriminatory nutrition
• Discriminatory
  health care

Postreproductive years
(45+ years)

• Cardiovascular
  diseases
• Gynecological
  cancers
• Osteoporosis
• Osteoarthritis
• Diabetes

Lifetime Health
Problems

• Gender violence
• Certain occupational
  and environmental
  health hazards
• Depression

Adolescence
(10–19 years)

• Early childbearing
• Abortion
• STDs and AIDS
• Undernutrition and
  micronutrient
  deficiency
• Rising trend in
  substance abuse

Reproductive years
(20–44 years)

• Unplanned pregnancy
• STDs and AIDS
• Abortion
• Pregnancy complications
• Malnutrition, especially
  iron deficiency

Note: The adolescent years are broken out separately here, although the usual distinction is between children
(ages 5–14) and those of reproductive age (15–44).

Sex selection.   In countries where many families have a strong prefer-
ence for sons, there is evidence of selective abortion of female fetuses (whose
sex is detected by ultrasound and amniocentesis) and of female infanticide
(Heise, Pitanguy, and Germain 1994). In Bombay, India, only one of 8,000
abortions performed after parents learned the sex of the fetus averted the birth
of a male (UN 1991).

Genital mutilation.   Each year an estimated 2 million young girls are subjected to genital mutilation, also known as female circumcision (see Box 3.2).

FIGURE 2.2 RATIO OF FEMALE TO MALE MORTALITY FOR CHILDREN AGED 1–4,
SELECTED COUNTRIES

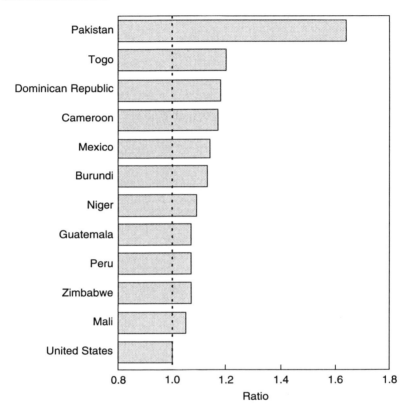

Source: Demographic and health surveys for Burundi (1987), Cameroon (1991), the Dominican Republic
(1991), Guatemala (1987), Mali (1987), Mexico (1987), Niger (1992), Pakistan (1990–91), Peru (1992),
Togo (1988), and Zimbabwe (1988–89); Keyfitz and Flieger 1990 for the United States.

Often performed under unsterile conditions, this invasive procedure can lead
to death, acute pain, recurrent urinary tract infections, mental trauma, painful
intercourse, and complications during childbirth (Acsadi and Johnson-Acsadi
1993; WHO 1993b).

Adolescence

Although women aged 10 to 19 are generally healthy, their emerging sexuality and exposure to a variety of risks during the transition from childhood to

adulthood can jeopardize their survival and well-being. Their status within the family and community is at its lowest in most countries during this phase of the life cycle. To a large extent, adolescence sets the stage for health and nutritional status in the later years, yet health policies and programs are the least effective in addressing the needs of this age group.

Early childbearing. The proportion of women giving birth during their teenage years ranges from 10 to 50 percent. Early childbearing is particularly common in traditional, often rural, settings where early marriage is the norm, but it is becoming increasingly prevalent among unmarried adolescents. In some settings a young girl may welcome an early premarital pregnancy to demonstrate her fertility or to motivate a partner to commit to marriage. Regardless of whether or not premarital sexuality is condemned, early pregnancy can have particularly harmful effects on a girl's social and economic opportunities. In Botswana, for example, a study found that one in seven women who dropped out of school did so because of pregnancy, and of those, only one in five returned to school (Bledsoe and Cohen 1993).

Adolescent girls are not physically prepared for childbirth, since linear growth is not complete until age 18 and the birth canal does not reach mature size until two to three years later (UN ACC/SCN 1992). As a result of this and other factors, teenage mothers face a high risk of serious pregnancy-related complications. In a Nigerian study, for example, 17 percent of 14-year-olds developed hypertensive disorders of pregnancy, compared with 3 percent of women aged 20 to 34. Also in Nigeria, 33 percent of all cases of fistulae (a tearing of the walls between the vagina and bladder or rectum following prolonged labor) involve women under age 16 (WHO 1989).

Adolescents also face at least a 20 percent greater likelihood of maternal or infant death than women in their twenties. The risks increase severalfold for women under age 16. Despite their high risk, most unmarried adolescents lack the requisite knowledge and services to prevent pregnancy. Studies in Guatemala and Kenya found that fewer than one in ten unmarried youths could correctly identify the fertile period (CDC 1991; Ajayi and others 1991). In most developing countries a majority of young women have heard of at least one modern contraceptive method, but they generally do not have adequate knowledge about correct usage. National surveys in several African countries found that although at least one in four women aged 15 to 19 was single and sexually experienced, few were using contraception. Among those who were using contraception, large proportions were relying on ineffective traditional methods such as rhythm and withdrawal (Population Reference Bureau 1992; Yinger and others 1992).

Unsafe abortion.   Many unmarried adolescents seek abortions—whether legal or not—to avoid expulsion from school and social condemnation. Because they often seek clandestine abortions and delay in obtaining the procedure and seeking attention for associated problems, adolescents have a higher rate of abortion complications. Studies of hospital records in several African countries found that between 38 and 68 percent of women seeking care for complications of abortion were under 20 years of age.

STDs, including AIDS.   STDs are spreading rapidly among young women, mainly through liaisons with older men and prostitution. In Thailand, for example, an estimated 800,000 prostitutes are under age 20, one-quarter are under 14, and roughly three in ten are HIV-infected (IPPF 1992). There is evidence that adolescent girls are biologically more vulnerable to STDs than older women, and they are likely to have more difficulty negotiating safe sex practices with their partners. In parts of Africa, HIV infection is increasing more rapidly among females than males, especially among adolescent girls (Panos Institute 1989). Studies in Ethiopia and Zimbabwe reveal that while the ratio of HIV infection is equal among men and women aged 20 to 29, girls aged 15 to 19 are three to five times more likely than boys to be infected (Zewdie 1993). On average, women become infected five to ten years earlier than men (UNDP 1993).

Undernutrition and micronutrient deficiency.   Girls' nutritional needs increase in early adolescence because of the growth spurt associated with puberty and the onset of menstruation. Inadequate diet during this period can jeopardize girls' health and physical development, with lifelong consequences. Iron-deficiency anemia is particularly common among adolescent girls. Skeletal growth is also delayed by malnutrition, and since a smaller pelvis can prolong labor and obstruct delivery, incomplete skeletal growth, or stunting, poses serious risks during childbirth.

Increased substance abuse.   Adolescents often experiment with harmful substances, including tobacco, alcohol, and drugs. Diseases associated with lifestyle and behavior have been less of a problem for women than for men, but this is changing in some countries. Cigarette advertising is now targeting women and young people, and smoking is spreading most rapidly among young women. Early initiation of such behaviors sets a pattern for lifelong use and increases morbidity and mortality, including risks specific to women's reproductive functions. For example, women over age 30 who smoke heavily and take oral contraceptives have a higher risk of cardiovascular disease, and pregnant women who smoke have a higher risk of stillbirth, premature labor, and low-birthweight babies.

Reproductive Years

Women's risk of premature death and disability is greatest during their reproductive years. And many conditions that have their onset during this period continue to affect the health of women—and that of their children—long after their reproductive years are over.

Unplanned pregnancy and abortion. Unplanned pregnancy is common in every country. In most developing countries, about 20 to 30 percent of married women—or about 120 million women—wish to avoid becoming pregnant but are not using contraception (Westoff and Ochoa 1991). This number would increase substantially if unmarried women, women who need a better or more suitable contraceptive method, and women who use abortion services were included. One in five births in these countries is unwanted.

Worldwide, an estimated 40 million to 60 million women resort to abortion to end unwanted pregnancies. Because the majority of abortions are unsafe, the procedure carries a high risk of injury and death, accounting for 125,000 to 200,000 female deaths annually (Dixon-Mueller 1990; Rosenfield 1989; WHO 1992c). Abortion-related mortality is highest in countries where abortion is legally restricted, access to family planning and safe abortion services is limited, and overall maternal mortality is high. About 40 percent of the world's population lives in countries with no restrictions on abortion, 23 percent where abortion is permitted for social and medical reasons, 12 percent where abortion is permitted when the woman's life and health are at stake or there are injuries to the fetus, and 25 percent where abortion is permitted only to save the life of the woman or is not permitted at all (Henshaw 1990). The cost of treating abortion-related complications is much greater than the cost of safe abortion.

Pregnancy-related complications. Each year more than 150 million women become pregnant, more than 50 million experience acute pregnancy-related complications, and 15 million develop long-term disabilities (WHO 1992a). Half a million of these women die as a result. In developing countries more than one-fourth of all deaths of women of reproductive age are pregnancy-related, caused mainly by hemorrhage, sepsis, unsafe abortion, hypertensive disorders, and obstructed labor. While maternal mortality has fallen in parts of Latin America and in Southeast and West Asia, it remains high in Africa and South Asia. Even though the risk of dying as a result of pregnancy or childbirth has declined globally, the number of pregnancy-related deaths has continued to rise as the number of women in their prime childbearing years also rises.

In addition, conditions such as malaria, viral hepatitis, diabetes, anemia, sickle cell disease, tuberculosis, and rheumatic heart disease are aggravated by pregnancy (WHO 1992a). Disabilities resulting from pregnancy include genital or bladder prolapse, cervical lacerations, obstetric fistulae, anemia, and infertility. In Colombia, Pakistan, the Philippines, and Syria, between 9 and 25 percent of women under age 45 suffer uterine prolapse (Omran and Standley 1976, 1981).

Malnutrition.   An estimated 450 million adult women in developing countries are stunted as a result of protein-energy malnutrition during childhood (World Bank 1993b). As Figure 2.3 illustrates, more than 50 percent of pregnant women in the developing world are anemic (WHO 1992c). About 250 million women suffer the effects of iodine deficiency, and, although the exact numbers are unknown, millions are probably blind due to vitamin A deficiency (Leslie 1991). The highest levels of malnutrition among women are found in South Asia (DeMaeyer and Adiels-Tegman 1985), where 60 percent

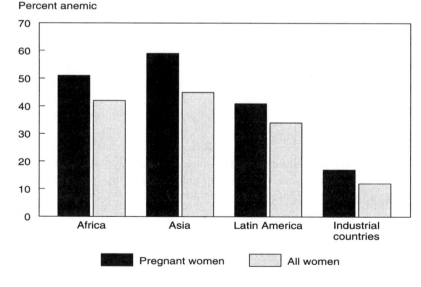

FIGURE 2.3 PREVALENCE OF ANEMIA AMONG WOMEN AGED 15–49 (1990)

Percent anemic

Source: WHO 1992c.

of women of reproductive age are underweight, more than 60 percent are anemic, and 15 percent are stunted (UN ACC/SCN 1992). The causes of malnutrition include inadequate food supply, inequitable distribution of food within the household, improper food storage and preparation, taboos against eating certain foods, and lack of knowledge about nutritious foods. Malnutrition hampers women's productivity, increases their susceptibility to infections, and contributes to numerous debilitating and fatal conditions.

STDs, including AIDS.	Most reproductive tract infections (RTIs) are sexually transmitted. RTIs are of three types: STDs, infections such as candidiasis and bacterial vaginosis caused by overgrowth of vaginal organisms, and infections associated with unhygienic practices. Women are not only more susceptible to these infections than men, but also more likely to be asymptomatic women and to experience complications from untreated RTIs. RTIs can cause pelvic inflammatory disease, infertility, adverse pregnancy outcomes, and chronic pain. Among STDs, HIV/AIDS and syphilis may directly result in death. Other STDs, however, can lead to life-threatening complications such as ectopic pregnancy and cervical cancer.

RTIs are common in all developing countries. In Egypt, for example, a recent community-based study found that over one-half of the women sampled had one or more RTIs (Younis and others 1993).

HIV/AIDS, which is primarily transmitted sexually, is spreading rapidly among women (see Figure 2.4). This is particularly true in Sub-Saharan Africa, where nearly 4 million adult women are already infected and where more than 13 million women may be infected by the year 2000 (WHO 1993c). Women with HIV run a high risk of passing the virus to their newborns, and they usually die while their children are still growing up. Tests of one-year-old babies of HIV-infected mothers showed that between 15 and 40 percent were also HIV-positive (WHO 1992b).

A number of factors place women at greater risk than men of contracting HIV/AIDS. Women are more likely to become infected each time they are exposed, because they have more mucosal surface exposed during sexual intercourse, and semen contains a much higher concentration of HIV than vaginal fluid. Women are also more likely than men to have asymptomatic, untreated STDs, which increases their susceptibility to HIV infection. Furthermore, women's sex partners tend to be older than they are and thus more likely to be infected. In addition, social norms that require female passivity and economic dependence on men make it difficult for women to insist on mutual fidelity or condom use (WHO 1993c). Finally, women may be exposed to HIV infection when they receive blood transfusions to combat pregnancy-related anemia or hemorrhage.

FIGURE 2.4 ESTIMATED CUMULATIVE HIV INFECTIONS IN WOMEN BY EARLY 1994

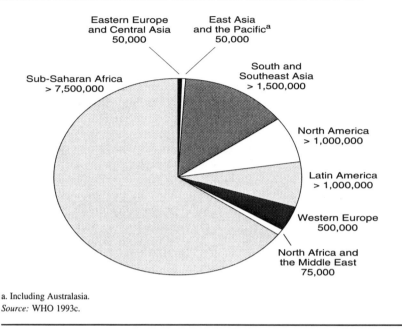

a. Including Australasia.
Source: WHO 1993c.

Postreproductive Years

By the year 2020, one in five women in developing countries will be 50 or older. As a result of urbanization, migration, and changing family structure, women are increasingly neglected in their old age. The cumulative effects of a lifetime of nutritional deprivation, hazardous and heavy work, continuous childbearing, and low self-esteem leaves them both physically and mentally frail, while abandonment and widowhood often leave them destitute. Because of their tendency to marry men older than themselves, as well as their longer life expectancy, women are more likely than men to be widowed. With the shift away from the support of extended families, elderly women are increasingly left on their own. Loss of a partner and living alone may have important health implications.

Most of the problems affecting women after the age of 45 are chronic. Injuries and infections (particularly tuberculosis) also contribute to women's disability in their later years, as do malnutrition, anemia, and loss of visual acuity. Menopause leads to alterations in the skeletal, cardiovascular, nervous, skin, genitourinary, and gastrointestinal systems and can affect women's capacity to perform everyday activities. The health problems of postmenopausal women, however, continue to be largely ignored.

Gynecological cancers.   These may occur during the reproductive years, but they are more prevalent after age 40. Cancers of the cervix and breast are the most common. Although cervical cancer can be cured at a relatively low cost if detected early, 183,000 women in developing countries die from it every year (Sherris and others 1993; World Bank 1993b). Breast cancer, which kills 158,000 women in developing countries each year, requires more sophisticated screening and treatment techniques (World Bank 1993b).

Cardiovascular and cerebrovascular diseases.   Cardiovascular diseases, including ischemic heart disease, myocardial infarction, and cerebrovascular disease (stroke), are the leading cause of death among adults age 45 and older in developing countries and represent a higher proportion of the disease burden among women than men in this age group (World Bank 1993b). With the increasing prevalence among women of risk-producing behaviors (such as smoking and alcohol consumption), the incidence of cardiovascular disease is expected to rise.

Diabetes.   Among urban women in Asia, the Middle East, and Latin America and the Caribbean, where obesity and inadequate exercise are becoming more common, the prevalence of diabetes mellitus is growing. Diabetes is a major cause of morbidity and can lead to blindness, kidney damage, and damage to the lower limbs.

Undernutrition.   In the poorer developing countries, chronic malnutrition is common among women, often reflecting a lifetime of inadequate intake of calories, vitamins, and minerals. In times of food shortage, elderly women are often most adversely affected.

Osteoporosis.   Worldwide, one in ten women over age 60 has osteoporosis, a process of bone loss that may result in pain, disability, and increased risk of fractures. Osteoporosis is most common in women beyond reproductive age because bone loss rises sharply after menopause. Insufficient calcium, inadequate exercise, smoking, and excessive consumption of alcohol are contributing factors.

Osteoarthritis.   During and after menopause, women are particularly prone to the development of osteoarthritis, a painful degenerative joint disease. Typically, several joints are affected, and progression of the disease restricts the performance of even routine activities. Repeated trauma to the joints has been identified as a predisposing factor, and obesity can exacerbate the condition.

Additional Health Problems

Some health problems that affect both men and women during the life cycle have a disproportionate effect on women because of cultural norms or differences in exposure or in access to treatment. Three of the major types of health problems that have a differential impact on women are described below.

Gender-based violence.   Men are often victims of street violence, brawls, homicide, and crime, but violence directed at women is a distinctly different phenomenon. Men tend to be attacked and killed by strangers or casual acquaintances, whereas women are most at risk at home and from men whom they know. Violence against women also tends to be acute, less likely to be reported, and often associated with sexual abuse.

Domestic violence, rape, and sexual abuse are widespread in virtually all regions, classes, cultures, and age groups. Reliable data on the incidence of rape are difficult to obtain, as many rapes go unreported. Among women aged 18 to 21 in five countries, however, between 8 and 18 percent of those surveyed reported that they had been raped (Heise, Pitanguy, and Germain 1994). Sexual abuse can occur at any time during the life cycle, but studies suggest that an alarming proportion of victims of rape and incest are 10 years old or younger. Other forms of violence against girls and women include female infanticide, forced prostitution, dating and courtship violence, marital rape, and abuse of widows and elderly women.

In addition to affecting women's health care–seeking behavior (abusive husbands often prevent women from seeking care), gender-based victimization can lead to unwanted pregnancy, infection, miscarriage, gynecological problems, depression, and many other forms of partial or permanent disability. Not infrequently, victims of battering and sexual assault attempt suicide (Heise, Pitanguy, and Germain 1994).

Of women surveyed in various countries, between 20 and 60 percent report having been beaten by their partners (World Bank 1993b). Recent estimates of the global burden of disease indicate that women of reproductive age in industrial countries lose one out of five healthy days of life because of domestic violence and rape; their counterparts in developing countries lose one out of twenty days (World Bank 1993b). The health burden of gender violence among women of reproductive age is comparable to that of other conditions already high on the world agenda. Reducing violence against women would therefore help reduce health care expenditures, as well as address this violation of basic human rights.

Depression.   In general, men and women aged 15 to 44 are about equally likely to suffer neuropsychiatric problems. However, depressive disorders are responsible for 5.8 percent of all deaths and disabilities among women of reproductive age—twice the rate among men (World Bank 1993b). Suicide accounts for an additional 3 percent of deaths among women in this age group, more than are caused by either respiratory infections or motor vehicle accidents (World Bank 1993b). Depression is the single most serious mental problem for women in every age group, and it has a significant impact on women's well-being and productivity (Paltiel 1993). *World Development Report 1993* (World Bank 1993b) ranks depressive disorders and self-inflicted injuries fifth and sixth, respectively, among the diseases and injuries most affecting women aged 15 to 44. Factors that put women at risk of depression include their inferior social and economic status, physical or sexual abuse, infertility, the conflicting demands of their domestic and income-producing roles, and, particularly among elderly women, isolation.

Certain occupational and environmental health hazards.   While men and women alike may be exposed to many occupational and environmental health hazards, some have particular effects on women. Because many women work in the home, they suffer disproportionately from inadequate water supply, poor sanitation, and indoor air pollution. A study in India found that rural women cooking in poorly ventilated huts were exposed to 100 times the acceptable level of suspended smoke particles—six times higher than other household members (Chatterjee 1991).

Outside the home, women workers may face the risk of sexual harassment and rape. Furthermore, they are more likely than men to work in industries and small enterprises with unsafe working conditions and poor regulation of such hazards as toxic chemicals, radiation, extreme temperatures, excessive noise, and violence. Electronic assembly workers report a loss of visual acuity, and textile workers complain of pulmonary problems, dermatitis, hand injuries, and chronic back pain (Hovell and others 1988). Exposure to toxic chemicals can cause cancer, dermatitis, miscarriage, and birth defects. Women may be particularly susceptible to some toxic chemicals for biological reasons (Rovner 1993).

Most women in developing countries are employed in low-wage positions—for example, as food vendors, petty traders, and domestic workers; they cannot afford to purchase health care or protective clothing and equipment. Many women farmers, especially those in commercial agriculture, are regularly exposed to pesticides, often without appropriate safeguards.

When pregnant women are exposed to many of these hazards, the health of their unborn children suffers as well. Heavy work during pregnancy can lead to premature labor and, when high energy demands are not compensated by increased caloric intake, to low-birthweight babies.

CHAPTER THREE

Health and Nutrition
Interventions for Women

Because the factors that affect women's well-being and productivity cover a wide spectrum, policymakers and program planners have to make difficult decisions about priorities. To provide a rational basis for making such choices, this chapter begins by describing a minimum package of women's health interventions that should be priorities for most developing countries. It then presents a set of expanded interventions that can be instituted as resources permit. The interventions included in both packages were selected for their impact in reducing female disability and death, their affordable cost, and their feasibility in developing countries (see the Appendix). Although estimates of cost-effectiveness are not widely available for education and communication efforts, such measures are described because of their strong potential for influencing health-related attitudes and practices.

The essential services for women's health confer widespread economic and social benefits of sufficient importance to justify public funding. Many of these interventions relate to women's reproductive and sexual health.

The expanded services comprise interventions that can be implemented by middle-income countries (and by poorer countries to the extent that funds permit) to reap even more gains. They are primarily enhancements of the essential services, interventions for women beyond reproductive age, and interventions to promote behavioral change in order to prevent health and nutrition problems and reduce gender discrimination and violence.

Although the two sets of recommended interventions are beneficial to all women, specific strategies will need to be tailored to the particular economic, epidemiological, demographic, and infrastructural conditions of each country or local setting. The cultural and socioeconomic factors that affect women's lives must also be taken into account when prioritizing interventions and planning delivery strategies. Potentially cost-effective devices for disease prevention, such as condoms, sometimes fail in practice because social mores prevent women from negotiating their use.

Essential Health Interventions

Essential health interventions fall into three categories: prevention and management of unwanted pregnancies, pregnancy services, and prevention and management of STDs (Table 3.1).

Prevention and Management of Unwanted Pregnancies

Preventing unwanted pregnancies improves women's health by reducing their exposure to the complications of pregnancy, childbirth, and unsafe abortion. In addition, the survival chances of children are significantly influenced by the timing and spacing of births, as well as by overall family size. Health services can best address the problem of unwanted pregnancy by providing family planning services and—where national policies permit—safe services for termination of pregnancy.

Family planning services.   Where fertility and mortality rates are high, family planning alone can have a substantial impact on maternal mortality. For example, in a rural subdistrict of Bangladesh, the maternal mortality rate fell by about one-third following an effective community-based project that raised contraceptive prevalence to more than 50 percent, compared with 23 percent in the control area (Fauveau 1991). Providing family planning services costs, on average, only $15 to $150 per DALY saved in low-income countries (about $20 per contraceptive user) and is one of the most cost-effective health interventions. In countries where both mortality and fertility are still relatively high, the cost per child death prevented is also extremely low. In Mali, for example, it averages about $130, or $4 to $5 per DALY gained (World Bank 1993b).

Programs should provide high-quality, consumer-oriented family planning services that promote informed reproductive choice. Because contraceptive needs and preferences change throughout a woman's life, a good selection of short- and long-term methods should be provided. Health agencies should establish a variety of service-delivery points and encourage commercial outlets

TABLE 3.1 ESSENTIAL SERVICES FOR WOMEN'S HEALTH

Essential health interventions	*Essential interventions for behavioral change*

PREVENTION AND MANAGEMENT OF UNWANTED PREGNANCIES

- Family planning
- Management of complications from unsafe abortion
- Termination of pregnancy

PREGNANCY SERVICES

Prenatal care
- Prompt detection, management, and referral of pregnancy complications
- Tetanus toxoid immunization
- Iron and folate supplements
- Iodine supplements, where warranted
- Malaria prophylaxis in infested areas

Safe delivery
- Hygienic routine delivery
- Detection, management, and referral of obstetric complications
- Facility-based obstetric care

Postpartum care
- Monitoring for infection and hemorrhage

PREVENTION AND MANAGEMENT OF SEXUALLY TRANSMITTED DISEASES

- Condom promotion and distribution
- Prenatal screening and treatment for syphilis
- Symptomatic case management
- Screening and treatment of commercial sex workers

PROMOTION OF POSITIVE HEALTH PRACTICES

- Laws, education, and services to encourage delayed childbearing among adolescents
- Counseling and public education to promote safe sex
- Public education and programs to ensure adequate nutrition
- Strategic efforts to increase male involvement in women's health issues

ELIMINATION OF HARMFUL PRACTICES

- Public education and services to discourage gender discrimination, domestic violence, and rape
- Policy dialogue and public education to discourage female genital mutilation

to offer contraceptives for sale at reasonable cost. Condoms, oral contraceptives, and spermicides can be made available immediately, even in resource-poor settings, since they can be provided by community-based distributors with appropriate training and sold through commercial outlets. Trained paramedical workers (nurses and midwives) can safely provide most other methods, including injectables, implants, intrauterine devices (IUDs), and voluntary sterilization.

Breastfeeding also plays an important role in child spacing and can complement other family planning methods. During the first six months after giving birth, a woman who is amenorrheic (having no menses) and feeding her baby only breastmilk receives 98 percent protection against pregnancy (Georgetown University School of Medicine 1990). Infants also derive health benefits from exclusive breastfeeding for the first six months and from breastmilk supplemented with other food for up to a year and a half thereafter. Health workers at all levels should encourage mothers to breastfeed and consume an adequate diet to meet the added nutritional needs that breastfeeding demands.

Making contraceptives widely available can greatly reduce the incidence of unsafe abortion. In Santiago, Chile, for example, deaths and hospitalization for complications from abortion fell dramatically after free IUD insertions were offered in 1964. As contraceptives became increasingly available throughout Chile, abortion-related deaths and complication rates plummeted (Figure 3.1). Safer abortion, although still illegal, may also have played a role.

Management of complications from unsafe abortion and safe services for terminating pregnancy. Women's health care can be greatly improved by timely and appropriate treatment of abortion complications, as well as providing postcoital contraception and safe termination of pregnancy. Complications from unsafe abortion (hemorrhage, shock, and sepsis) are often life-threatening and costly to treat, requiring emergency referral, two to three days of hospital care, anesthesia, antibiotics, surgery, and blood transfusion. Vacuum aspiration abortion, provided by a trained health worker early in pregnancy, is up to a thousand times safer than clandestine abortion (Johnson, Benson, and Hawkins 1992). Safe abortion is one of the most cost-effective measures for reducing maternal death and disability.

Abortion during the first trimester and treatment of incomplete abortion without complications can be handled safely at primary-level health centers on an outpatient basis by trained nurses, midwives, or paramedics using vacuum aspiration (McLaurin, Hord, and Wolfe 1991; Rosenfield 1989). Dilation and curettage requires more surgical skill and anesthetic support. Health facilities that provide abortions or treat complications arising from unsafe abortions can realize substantial savings by using vacuum aspiration. In one year a single Kenyan hospital saved an estimated $300,000—equal to the annual salaries for

FIGURE 3.1 RATES OF CONTRACEPTIVE USE AND OF DEATH OR HOSPITALIZATION FROM ABORTION COMPLICATIONS, CHILE, 1964–78

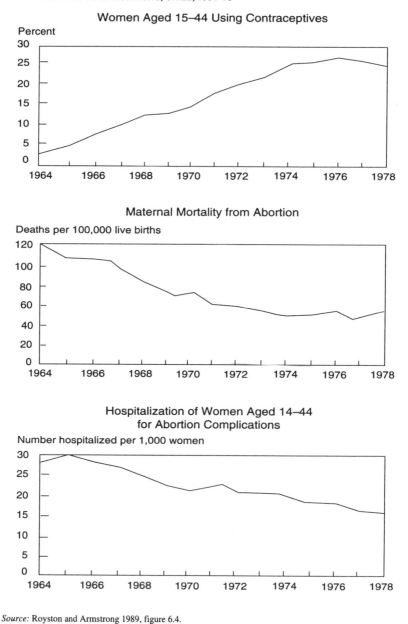

Source: Royston and Armstrong 1989, figure 6.4.

200 nurses—by switching from dilation and curettage to vacuum aspiration to treat incomplete abortions (Kizza and Rogo 1990). Reducing the incidence of incomplete abortions would lower hospital costs even more. Following an abortion, women should receive counseling, services, and referrals as needed to ensure they have the means to prevent unwanted pregnancy in the future.

Where abortion is legal but not widely available (as in India), programs should strive to increase access by expanding services, delegating responsibility, and training mid-level providers. In areas where abortion is routinely used for birth control (as in parts of Eastern Europe and Central Asia), programs need to increase the availability of contraceptives and to provide postabortion family planning information and services.

Pregnancy Services

Safe pregnancy services are designed to ensure timely detection, management, and referral of complications during pregnancy, labor, and delivery. About one in three pregnant women develop complications requiring treatment from a trained provider, and one in ten require hospitalization. (A more detailed discussion of pregnancy-related services can be found in Tinker and Koblinsky 1993.)

Because of their impact on the health of the child as well as the mother, safe pregnancy services are highly cost-effective. Providing prenatal, delivery, and postpartum services costs less than $2,000 per death averted, or between $30 and $250 per DALY saved (World Bank 1993b). In resource-poor countries, priority should be given to improving hygienic practices, providing iron and folate supplementation, and strengthening linkages and referral services for obstetric complications.

Prenatal care.   Regular prenatal care is needed to help detect and manage some pregnancy-related complications (such as pre-eclampsia, infection, and obstructed labor) and to educate women about danger signs, potential complications, and where to seek help. In Ethiopia and Nigeria, nurse-midwives working with traditional birth attendants referred short women having their first birth to the hospital for delivery. This program substantially reduced the number of maternal deaths from obstructed labor. Prenatal care also provides an opportunity to offer preventive care that will benefit the infant as well as the mother (such as counseling on hygiene, breastfeeding, nutrition, family planning, tetanus toxoid immunization, and iron and folate supplementation) and to treat existing diseases that may be aggravated by pregnancy (such as malaria). Unfortunately, there is no established protocol for either the content or the timing of prenatal care. This is an issue of concern for any maternal health program and deserves immediate attention.

Because most pregnancy-related complications cannot be anticipated, all women need access to appropriate care should complications develop. In Ethiopia, for example, maternity waiting homes have been established near hospitals to bring women living in remote areas to obstetric care before the expected due date (Brennan 1992; Poovan, Kifle, and Kwast 1990).

Because newborns and mothers can contract tetanus from nonsterile delivery procedures, immunization against tetanus is especially important for women who deliver in nonmedical settings. Immunizing pregnant women against tetanus costs less than $6 per DALY saved, based on infant deaths averted (Jamison 1993).

The regular intake of iron and folate tablets can prevent or cure anemia among pregnant and lactating women. Providing iron supplementation for pregnant women is highly cost-effective, at a cost of less than $2 to $4 per person annually, or less than $13 per DALY saved, based on infant deaths averted (World Bank 1993b). Iron pills should be routinely provided to pregnant women and properly stored to protect quality. Pills can also be made available through community-based distribution and commercial outlets. Training for health care providers and consumer education can improve patient compliance. Fortification of commonly used foods (salt or sugar) with iron, iodine, and vitamin A is even more cost-effective than supplementation.

Where iodine deficiency is endemic, providing iodized oil to women of reproductive age is a low-cost addition to existing maternal and child health services, particularly where iodized salt is not available. The most effective long-term approach to reducing iodine deficiency is iodization of salt for the whole community. Use of injected or oral iodized oil every two to five years among women of reproductive age costs less than $19 per DALY saved, based on child deaths averted (World Bank 1993b).

At about the fourteenth week of gestation, especially in a first pregnancy, women's resistance to malaria begins to diminish. While providing bed nets and antimalarial drugs to pregnant women in infested areas can prevent severe illness and reduce the associated risk of low-birthweight infants (Steketee 1989), prompt diagnosis and proper treatment of malaria during pregnancy may be the most cost-effective course of action.

Safe delivery.   Delivery care should include safe management of routine deliveries, safe-birth kits for traditional birth attendants, communication and transport to ensure timely referral and management of emergency complications, and essential obstetric functions at the first-referral level.

Health agencies should be able to ensure hygienic routine delivery in the community by trained paramedics, particularly midwives, or traditional birth attendants. Most postpartum hemorrhage, which is largely unpredictable, can be prevented if skilled birth attendants effectively manage the third stage of labor. Sepsis at delivery can be largely prevented by minimizing vaginal examinations and ensuring clean delivery practices. When rupture of the membranes occurs long before labor, antibiotics should be provided.

Most life-threatening complications occur during labor and delivery, and because most of these cannot be predicted, every woman needs access to emergency obstetric care. Effective treatment of hemorrhage often includes rapid manual removal of retained placenta, oxytocic drugs, intravenous fluids, blood transfusion, and surgery. In cases of hemorrhage, obstructed labor, and other obstetrical emergencies, the most important element in a woman's treatment may be transportation. Death from hemorrhage, for example, usually occurs within two hours of onset. When distance is a factor, first aid at the community or health center level may be necessary to save a woman's life by stabilizing her condition until she reaches the hospital. Advance planning for emergencies is therefore key to reducing maternal mortality.

Specially trained staff are needed to perform some obstetrical procedures (cesarean section and symphysiotomy for obstructed labor, laparotomy or hysterectomy to stop persistent bleeding, treatment for eclampsia and sepsis, and repair of obstetric fistulae). In Zaire, women's lives have been saved by nurses trained to perform cesarean sections (White, Thorpe, and Maine 1987).

Efforts must also be made to improve existing services. Major barriers to utilization include long distances to health facilities, inadequate transportation, lack of funds to pay for transport and health care, lack of knowledge about the benefits of formal health care, and low-quality care.

Postpartum care. Postpartum care should include early detection and management of infection and hemorrhage, support for exclusive breastfeeding for six months, nutrition counseling, and family planning services. Even among women who have delivered in a hospital, postpartum follow-up is important because complications may arise after leaving inpatient care. Educating women, their families, birth attendants, and community health workers to recognize early signs of and seek care for infection, for example, may be lifesaving. Antibiotic treatment is sufficient to cure infection in more than 80 percent of cases if taken within four days of the onset of fever (Winikoff and others 1991).

Postpartum care should respond to women's needs and preferences to ensure utilization and effectiveness. In Tunisia the innovative Sfax program delivers integrated family planning and health services to the mother and child by linking postpartum care with a cultural tradition. In addition to follow-up and counseling immediately after birth, the program provides health services and information for the mother and the infant on the fortieth day after birth, a day of religious and cultural importance for Tunisian mothers and children (Coeytaux 1989).

Prevention and Management of STDs

At the primary health care level, efforts to control STDs should focus on preventing transmission and treating infection in order to avert severe complications. Since the emergence of HIV/AIDS as a major public health problem and the identification of STDs as risk factors for its spread, primary prevention of STDs merits increasing attention.

Treating STDs costs only $1 to $55 per DALY saved (World Bank 1993b). Preventing a single STD case in a woman is estimated to be almost 20 percent more effective than preventing a single case in a man (Over and Piot 1993). Women are more susceptible to catching STDs from men than vice versa, and the severity of STDs (other than HIV) is generally greater in women than in men. In addition, preventing and curing STDs in women who are or may become pregnant reduces perinatal transmission.

The costs of treating STDs are much lower than the costs of treating their complications or the enormous direct and indirect costs of widespread STD and HIV infection (Piot and Rowley 1992). Although the lack of simple, inexpensive diagnostic tests for most STDs constrains control programs in areas with limited resources and facilities, syndromic diagnosis of STDs—based on characteristic groups of symptoms—can often be used in men and may be useful in symptomatic women.

Factors such as the emergence of antimicrobial resistance, the prevalence rate of STDs in the population, and the feasibility of reaching at-risk groups (including partner notification) must be considered when weighing program options. Health care providers should concentrate on making services available to high-frequency transmitters, particularly commercial sex workers, who contribute substantially to the spread of infection. The cost-effectiveness of interventions drops rapidly when they are directed at the general population. Where the infection has spread beyond high-risk groups, however, a broader approach is warranted.

Because contracepting and pregnant women are sexually active and therefore at risk, it is desirable and cost-effective to offer STD counseling, diagnosis, and treatment at clinics that also provide maternal and child health care and family planning. In addition, clustering of services is more cost-effective. Single-purpose STD programs often fail to reach women too embarrassed to use them and those who are asymptomatic or who fail to recognize symptoms.

Health workers at all levels—including traditional birth attendants—should be trained to recognize STD symptoms and to use appropriate treatment and referral protocols. Health workers should also be trained to counsel on condom use, identify sexual contacts, and assist in notification of partners when necessary.

Drugs for treating STDs should be included on national lists of essential drugs. Distribution should be encouraged through commercial channels and subsidized as necessary. Under a social marketing project in Cameroon, pharmacies sell an STD treatment kit containing antibiotics, instructions, a "partner referral" card to encourage partners to purchase the kit, STD information, and condoms (FHI 1992).

Condom promotion and distribution.   Aside from abstinence or changes in sexual behavior, condoms are the most effective means of preventing sexual transmission of STDs, including HIV/AIDS. To promote condom use, governments need to lower import duties and other fees (which typically raise condom prices by 35 to 100 percent) and permit condom advertising. Subsidizing condom distribution and promotion is estimated to cost $76 per DALY gained, taking into account how adults and children may be affected by STDs, AIDS, and cervical cancer (a secondary effect of some STDs). Factoring in family planning benefits reduces the cost per DALY gained (based on child outcomes) to $45, making condom distribution even more cost-effective (Jamison 1993).

To date, subsidized commercial sales, community-based distribution, and workplace programs have been effective means of distributing condoms to both high-risk groups and the general population. A community-wide intervention in Zimbabwe distributed more than 5.7 million condoms and reduced the incidence of STDs by 6 to 50 percent in different areas (World Bank 1993b). In Zaire a 1987 mass media and condom marketing program was highly effective: more than 80 percent of women surveyed had heard about AIDS on the radio, and condom sales rose to seven times previous levels in one year (Liskin and others 1989).

Prenatal screening and treatment for syphilis.   Cost-effectiveness estimates for treatment of syphilis vary greatly, depending upon its prevalence, assumptions about the risk of transmission, and the case-detection strategy used. In most developing countries, screening for syphilis using the Rapid Plasma Reagin test, which provides immediate results, followed by treatment with penicillin (where indicated), is a simple and inexpensive approach with significant payoffs for infant health (Schulz, Schulte, and Berman 1992). Accordingly, screening and treatment of syphilis during prenatal care is recommended. A project in Zambia reduced the incidence of syphilis among pregnant women by 60 percent within one year at a cost of $0.60 per prenatal screening and $12 per maternal syphilis case averted (Hira and others 1990).

The most serious consequence of gonorrhea and chlamydia in pregnant women is the occurrence of ophthalmia neonatorum, a severe eye infection that can cause blindness in newborns. Routine antibiotic prophylaxis for this condition in the newborn, which costs only $1.40 per case averted, is recommended rather than screening and treatment of all pregnant women (Schulz, Schulte, and Berman 1992).

Symptomatic case management.   Syndrome-based treatment of both urethral discharge (most commonly caused by gonorrhea and chlamydia) and genital ulcer diseases in symptomatic men is recommended. Symptomatic women with genital ulcers or pelvic inflammatory disease should also be diagnosed and treated using clinical algorithms developed by WHO. By following the step-by-step guidelines developed by WHO, health workers can match patient symptoms with those for locally prevalent STDs and provide treatment accordingly. Clinical and laboratory diagnosis of STDs is generally not feasible in low-resource countries, particularly in rural areas, because of cost and the unavailability of trained technical personnel and laboratory equipment (Lande 1993; Piot and Rowley 1992).

Targeted screening and treatment of commercial sex workers.   When targeted to frequent transmitters of infection, screening and treatment can be extremely cost-effective. A project to diagnose and treat STDs among prostitutes in Nairobi, for example, reduced the mean annual incidence of gonorrhea in this group from 2.85 cases per woman in 1986 to 0.66 cases per woman in 1989. The project also prevented an estimated 6,000 to 10,000 new cases of HIV infection, at approximately $8 to $12 per case, in addition to preventing other STDs (Moses and others 1991).

International efforts are now under way to develop rapid, accurate diagnostic methods for resource-poor settings and to introduce them into STD programs through the STD Diagnostics Initiative. Formed in 1990 by a group of STD experts from around the world, the initiative is developing quick, inexpensive tests for chlamydia, gonorrhea, and syphilis.

Essential Interventions for Behavioral Change

In addition to adopting the health care measures outlined above, countries can also benefit substantially from strategies to inform the public and change health-related behavior. Supportive health policies, including laws, government regulations, and health care protocols, are also essential.

Promoting Positive Health Practices

Information, education, and communication programs can change the attitudes and practices of men and women, health care providers, opinion leaders, and policymakers. Through broad education programs using mass media, community meetings, outreach workers, and other communication channels, health agencies can promote clinic attendance, educate consumers on healthy lifestyles and treatment alternatives, allay fears, refute false rumors, help shape social norms, and build a constituency for women's health and nutrition programs. Entertainment media have proven effective in promoting a variety of health-related behaviors, including family planning, AIDS prevention, better nutrition, and smoking cessation. Educational programs in clinic waiting areas reduce the time that doctors need to spend informing patients about health matters.

Public education programs and counseling teach women how to recognize the signs of disease and when and where to seek help. They can also enable women to treat minor ailments at home, while urging them to seek timely intervention at the first sign of serious problems. The promotion of specific household behaviors (such as washing hands and boiling water) can have a noticeable impact on the entire family's health. Teaching women and family members to recognize danger signs during pregnancy and to seek prompt medical attention can greatly reduce the incidence of maternal deaths. In Zaria, Nigeria, a radio campaign stressing the dangers of a labor lasting more than twenty-four hours is credited with a significant decrease in the incidence of obstetric fistulae (Harrison and others 1985).

Delayed childbearing among adolescents.   Laws and regulations have a major impact on the availability and accessibility of contraceptives and abortion. Where early marriage contributes to early childbearing, governments can raise the legal age of marriage and provide incentives for young women to postpone marriage and remain in school. Health workers can publicize the harmful effects of early childbearing and closely spaced pregnancies. Satisfied users of contraception can serve as peer motivators to reinforce these messages. Proscriptions regarding contraceptives and medical procedures and spousal consent requirements can be relaxed. Health agencies can have far more impact if they can ensure adolescents and unmarried women access to confidential reproductive and sexual health information and services, protected by law.

Programs need to target adolescents as a discrete group (Box 3.1). Messages, media use, outreach programs, and service outlets need to focus on adolescents' preferences and appeal to them directly. Whenever possible, adolescents should be involved in program planning. In general, education programs that are implemented by peers have been more effective than adult-directed initiatives. Multiservice centers that integrate recreation and education

---

BOX 3.1 REACHING ADOLESCENTS

When the Gente Joven ("Young People") program of the Mexican Family Planning Foundation was established in 1986, Mexican schools did not provide sex education. Gente Joven filled the gap by bringing information on sexuality and family planning to young people in poor urban areas. Its goals are to:

■ *Help teenagers make their own decisions, rather than simply provide them with contraceptives.* Gente Joven focuses on the emotional and social issues as well as the biological and clinical aspects of sexuality.

■ *Recognize gender differences that influence sexual activity and contraceptive use.* For example, a study on AIDS prevention revealed that girls are reluctant to bring up the subject of condom use because it might be interpreted by boys as evidence of too much sexual experience. Gente Joven incorporates such information into its program strategies.

■ *Focus on how ideas are communicated, as well as on what the message conveys.* Video and radio are widely used by Gente Joven because they are particularly effective channels for communicating with teenagers.

Source: Marques 1993.

---

with health services are effective in recruiting adolescents but may be costlier per contraceptive user than family planning clinics or outreach activities (Senderowitz forthcoming).

Schools should provide instruction in reproductive physiology and sex education—not only information on when conception occurs and how to prevent it, but also negotiating skills—as part of family life education or as an integral part of the school curriculum, starting before sexual activity has begun. Studies have shown that access to counseling and contraceptives does not encourage earlier or increased sexual activity (Grunseit and Kippax 1993).

Mass media campaigns can be effective in reaching adolescents. In Jamaica the National Family Planning Board broadcast television and radio spots and songs with the message, "Before you be a mother, you got to be a woman" (Church and Geller 1989). Yet while campaigns promoting delayed childbearing seem to be well received, there has been little analysis of their specific effects on behavior.

Safe sex.   Safe sex has been defined as sex that is safe from unwanted pregnancy, disease, and the unwanted use of power in sexual relationships (IPPF 1993). Because most people know little about STDs and HIV/AIDS transmission, symptoms, and long-term risks, public education programs need to explain why people should adopt preventive behaviors (including abstinence, monogamy, nonpenetrative sex, condom use, and other behaviors that reduce exposure) and why they should seek treatment. Despite some controversy, mass media campaigns have been effective in informing the public about STDs and AIDS and in changing sexual behavior. Following a nine-month mass media campaign in Mexico, for example, condom use rose among university students, prostitutes, and other audiences (Liskin and others 1989).

In general, women know less about STDs and AIDS than do men, learn about them later, and are less likely to hear about them from the mass media (Liskin and others 1989). Personal contacts with individual women or groups of women may be needed. Women can be approached at places where they usually meet, such as clinics, schools, market squares, and farms, or through grassroots organizations such as market women's associations and church groups (Post 1993). Education programs should reach women of all ages, including women of childbearing age, young girls who are not yet sexually active, and older women, who often educate and advise youth.

Counseling women in negotiating skills can help them persuade their partners to use condoms, and condom promotion campaigns can change men's negative image of condoms. Over the long term, fundamental attitudinal and behavioral change is needed to make gender relations more equitable, to ensure that women have more power to protect themselves against unwanted pregnancy and disease and that men share responsibility for the sexual health of their partners. Intensified research to develop effective female-controlled methods of STD prevention (such as a vaginal microbicide) is urgently needed.

Adequate nutrition. Health agencies can help inform people about women's nutritional needs at different stages of the life cycle and can promote better diets for girls and women. In addition, government agencies can identify the need for programs that address contributory problems, such as poverty, women's heavy workload, high fertility, lack of safe water supplies, and poor sanitation. Health workers can be trained to recognize nutritional deficiencies and to counsel patients on corrective measures. To be effective in countering harmful food taboos and changing food allocation patterns within households, messages must be tailored to local conditions.

High priority should be given to improving nutritional intake among young and adolescent girls in order to prevent health problems in later life. In areas where girls receive less or poorer-quality food than boys, health workers need to make an extra effort to educate caregivers on the long-term consequences of this practice. Special initiatives such as home visits, school meals, and other supplemental feeding programs may be helpful in improving girls' nutrition.

Even with little increase in household spending on food, nutrition education programs can influence food selection, preparation techniques, adherence to food prescriptions, use of vitamins and other supplements, and the treatment of diarrhea and other diseases that inhibit food absorption. Nutrition education programs have been successful in a variety of settings in promoting breastfeeding and appropriate weaning foods. They can also be used to promote low-cost, nutritious foods that are readily available and to encourage the cultivation of micronutrient-rich crops in home gardens as a way of ensuring an adequate supply of suitable foods. A project in West Sumatra, Indonesia, for example, promoted dark-green leafy vegetables (which are rich in iron and vitamin A) through the radio and other media. After the 1987–89 campaign, the proportion of pregnant women who consumed these vegetables daily rose from 19 to 32 percent (Favin and Griffiths 1991).

Increased male involvement and support.   In many cultures men make the decisions about such health-related concerns as food purchases and distribution within the family, family size, birth spacing, and the use of health care. In Senegal, for example, a study seeking to learn why so few women used maternal health services found that only 2 percent of the women interviewed said they would decide for themselves to seek care in the event of pregnancy-related complications. For most, the decision rested with their husbands (Thaddeus and Maine 1990). Education programs and services directed to men are needed to promote contraceptive use, safe sex, and reduction of substance abuse and violent behavior.

Health and other agencies need to make a concerted effort to make men aware of women's health problems and encourage them to take responsibility for the effects of their behavior. Reaching boys, both in and out of school, with reproductive health education is important because men so often dominate the sexual relationship. School-based and mass media programs that reach boys at a young age can be particularly effective in shaping later attitudes and practices.

To date, few health and nutrition education programs have been targeted to men. Examples of male-oriented programs are found in Honduras, Kenya, and Thailand, where breastfeeding campaigns urge the man to help his lactating wife by providing her with extra food and liquids and assuming extra chores to enable her to rest (Green 1989). In Mali a multimedia campaign was mounted to persuade men to provide women with additional and more nutritious foods during pregnancy (Fishman, Touré, and Gottert 1991).

To increase men's role in preventing unwanted pregnancy, family planning programs need to reach out to men to promote the use of male methods of contraception, support for their partner's contraceptive use, and increased spousal communication about family size, fertility regulation, and disease prevention. One approach is to establish hours or clinics for men only. PROFAMILIA, a

Colombian family planning association, has created men's clinics annexed to a longstanding program directed primarily to women. The clinics provide family planning and diagnosis and treatment of urological and sexual problems, infertility, and STDs (Rogow 1990).

The imbalance in contraceptive responsibility is particularly evident for voluntary sterilization. Despite the advantages of vasectomy over female sterilization—lower health risks, lower cost, and shorter recuperation time—female sterilization procedures predominate in nearly all countries. In Latin America, women obtain 93 percent of all sterilizations (PAHO 1993). Even in Thailand, where vasectomy has been heavily promoted, women obtain four in five sterilizations (Ross, Mauldin, and Miller 1993). The "no-scalpel" technique of vasectomy, which has further simplified the procedure, should be made more widely available and promoted. In addition, research is needed to provide a wider array of male contraceptive options.

Because women bear the major consequences of unplanned pregnancy, requiring men to meet their obligations might motivate them to take a more active role in preventing pregnancy. Few countries have policies requiring men to take financial responsibility for their offspring. Proposals for campaigns to promote male responsibility for family planning have generated useful public discussion. One poster featuring a doleful pregnant man asking, "Would you be more careful if it was you who got pregnant?" has been adapted for use in eight countries (Gallen, Liskin, and Kak 1986).

Eliminating Harmful Practices

In addition to educational and policy measures to promote positive health practices, governments and health agencies need to address harmful practices associated with women's subordinate status, such as discriminatory access to food and health care, genital mutilation, and gender violence. Because these practices arise from the social, economic, and cultural environment, cooperation and coordination on a wide scale are needed to change them.

By emphasizing the health aspects of harmful practices, governments can increase public awareness of their significance, prevalence, and impact. Health workers can be trained to recognize and treat the resulting health conditions, while health agencies can document them, identify their causes and potential interventions for their control, and disseminate related information.

Gender discrimination.   Health planners, managers, and providers can help sensitize policymakers, community leaders, and the general public about the profound impact that gender discrimination has on the health, well-being, and productivity of women. Public education programs on these topics can be provided as part of the essential services for women. Such programs should stress the high human costs of neglect and mistreatment of girls and women—including the long-term implications of inferior care for girls and the deleterious effects of poor nutrition and early childbearing.

While increasing public awareness is a necessary first step, the ultimate goal is the adoption of positive social norms and health behavior. Governments, therefore, will need to actively support interventions designed to change behaviors, first on a limited scale and later on the national level. Policies, cultural practices, and social norms that perpetuate women's low status need to be reexamined. Higher levels of education and vocational training for women, greater participation in the labor force, and improved access to income, land, and credit will also raise women's status and influence gender power relations.

Genital mutilation.   Governments and nongovernmental organizations (NGOs), including professional organizations and women's groups, should receive encouragement and material support to work for the elimination of genital mutilation. Laws and clear policy declarations prohibiting female genital mutilation may help, but more broadly based efforts are also needed. Widespread public education programs can publicize the harmful effects of genital mutilation and address its cultural roots. Local research may be needed to determine its prevalence, the cultural reasons for its perpetuation, and its consequences, as well as to test effective approaches for preventing it (Box 3.2). Health workers can help disseminate this information to the community.

Domestic violence and rape.   Violence against women is not just a health problem but a broad social problem, intertwined with gender power relations, sexuality, self-identity, and social institutions. It is therefore important not only to treat the physical and psychological injuries that result from violence, but also to examine the root causes and address the cultural and social legitimization of bodily harm and male control over female behavior.

In most countries, laws fail to protect the victims of domestic violence or to punish its perpetrators. Many violent crimes go unreported because the victim is afraid of the perpetrator and of society's skepticism, its condemnation of victims, and ostracism. Where violence against women is condoned or punished lightly, laws should be strengthened to serve as a deterrent. Key legal changes include removing barriers to prosecution (such as requirements for witnesses and evidence of permanent injury), eliminating practices that are prejudicial to women (for example, disregard of complaints by women who are not virgins and the exoneration of rapists who agree to marry their victims), and ensuring that married women have access to family assets and are free to leave abusive relationships.

BOX 3.2 ELIMINATING FEMALE GENITAL MUTILATION

Every year 2 million girls are subjected to genital mutilation. Unlike male circumcision, in which the foreskin is removed without damage to male organs, female circumcision involves the cutting and removal of parts or all of the external female genitals. Practiced mainly in Eastern and Western Africa, it is also found in parts of Asia and the Middle East (such as Egypt, India, and Yemen). Prevalence is highest in Somalia and Djibouti, where 98 percent of women are subject to genital mutilation, 80 percent or more of them in its most extreme form (Toubia 1993).

Genital mutilation has serious and sometimes fatal physical consequences, as well as psychological effects. The immediate consequences can include excruciating pain, hemorrhage, tetanus, and sepsis. The long-term consequences may include scarring, urinary tract infections, painful intercourse, obstetric fistulae, difficulty during urination and menstruation, and complications in childbirth.

Female genital mutilation has been discussed as both a human rights and a health issue. In 1990 the Convention of the Rights of the Child condemned female circumcision as torture and sexual abuse. The Forty-sixth World Health Assembly in 1992 adopted a resolution calling for the elimination of female genital mutilation and other harmful traditional practices. Organizations such as the Inter-African Committee on Traditional Practices Affecting the Health of Women and Children are working to focus attention on and eliminate female genital mutilation.

Because multiple cultural and social factors contribute to the continuation of this practice, it is best handled nationally, with the involvement of local women's and professional groups. In Burkina Faso a national committee to eradicate female genital mutilation was established in 1990 by presidential decree. The committee has established provincial groups, held workshops, and developed a film and teaching materials (IAC 1993).

In Kenya a study conducted by a women's organization, Maendeleo ya Wanawake Organization (MYWO), found that approximately 90 percent of the women interviewed had undergone genital mutilation. Even though most circumcised women reported having experienced problems, more than 65 percent expected to have their daughters circumcised. Additional qualitative research provided some explanations for this practice and belief. Circumcision signifies a rite of passage, conferring maturity and respectability. A girl who is uncircumcised is considered unfit to become a wife and mother. Benefits such as education, gifts, celebrations, and privileges are bestowed on the circumcised girl. MYWO has developed a communication program to reeducate community leaders, parents, elders, and youth, and it is exploring ways of eliminating the practice (Matovina 1992; Toubia 1993; WHO 1993b).

Health and family planning workers can be an important source of support and referral for victims of violence. They can, however, also exacerbate the situation through insensitive and judgmental behavior. Experience has shown that most women will discuss abuse if questioned by a sympathetic health care provider. Increasingly, specialized counseling, legal, and support services are available to assist abused women who are referred from health care settings. Even where no special services are available, health care providers can be trained to emphasize that no one deserves to be beaten or to be blamed for being raped.

In many countries, NGOs are raising awareness about violence against women. In Honduras, Jamaica, and Nicaragua, for example, NGOs have used theatrical productions to generate public discussion on this topic (Heise, Pitanguy, and Germain 1994; Popular Education Research Group 1992).

Expanded Health Interventions

For developing countries with the financial resources and political will to go beyond the essential services, the expanded services provide a more comprehensive set of interventions and therefore more adequate health services for women (Table 3.2). For low-income countries that initially adopt only the essential services, the expanded services can be incorporated incrementally.

Expansion of Essential Services

Increased choice of contraceptive methods. As family planning programs expand to cover more clients through a larger network of outlets, including intensified outreach to adolescents, so the range of contraceptive methods offered should expand. Each method added attracts new users and creates more choices for current users, increasing overall contraceptive prevalence and continuation rates and more successfully meeting women's differing needs. Analysis of data from seventy-two developing countries found that access to a range of methods strongly improved contraceptive prevalence (Freedman and Berelson 1976).

In settings with sufficient infrastructure, postcoital contraception can be used to help prevent unwanted pregnancy and reduce the need for abortion. The major postcoital methods are combination pills and IUDs, which have failure rates of under 2 percent if administered within three and five days of unprotected intercourse, respectively (Van Look 1990). A relatively new drug called RU-486, which can be used within the first sixty-three days of pregnancy in combination with a dose of prostaglandin, shows promise as a nonsurgical method of early abortion. The current regimen requires medical supervision,

TABLE 3.2 EXPANDED SERVICES FOR WOMEN'S HEALTH

Additional Health Interventions	Additional Interventions for Behavioral Change
EXPANSION AND IMPROVEMENT OF ESSENTIAL SERVICES	**INCREASED ATTENTION TO EARLY PREVENTION OF HEALTH PROBLEMS**
• Increased choice of contraceptive methods • Enhanced maternity care • Expanded screening for and treatment of sexually transmitted diseases • Extended nutrition assistance to vulnerable groups • Screening, treatment, and referral for victims of violence	• In-school education about reproductive physiology, sexuality, and reproductive health • Public information and services to prevent unwanted pregnancy and sexually transmitted diseases • Education about girls' special nutritional needs • Education to discourage smoking and substance abuse
CANCER SCREENING AND TREATMENT	**STRATEGIC EFFORTS TO REDUCE GENDER DISCRIMINATION AND VIOLENCE**
• For cervical cancer from age 35 • For breast cancer from age 50 (where resources permit)	• Public education initiatives • Training for health care workers • Networking within the community
	GREATER FOCUS ON WOMEN BEYOND REPRODUCTIVE AGE
	• Education about nutritional requirements • Self-help links with support networks

although alternatives are being studied. More information on the cost of RU-486 and on its infrastructural and medical backup requirements is needed before its widespread use can be advocated in low-income countries (Sundström 1993).

Enhanced maternity care. As the health infrastructure improves, maternity care services should be upgraded to include expanded routine and referral care, with increased coverage and full-service obstetric facilities. More detailed information on expanding maternity care services can be found in *Making Motherhood Safe* (Tinker and Koblinsky 1993).

With respect to prenatal care, increased attention needs to be given to the quality of care. Special efforts should be made to reach marginalized groups, such as adolescents. To improve the quality of care, maternal death audits should be introduced, and efforts should be intensified to coordinate supervision and backup from the hospital to the community level. Services will need to be decentralized, and women will need to be redirected to health centers for routine care, because referral sites will tend to become overwhelmed by demand. Birthing centers located near hospitals may provide a low-cost alternative for routine deliveries, as has been found in Mexico. As deliveries become increasingly institutionalized, providers need to resist the overuse or abuse of medical technologies such as cesarean sections (see Box 3.3) and to emphasize client-oriented care.

Expanded screening for and treatment of STDs. Health agencies can increase coverage for the screening and treatment of STDs as resources permit. Key interventions include the following:

■ *Expanded screening and treatment of high-frequency transmitters.* Intensified efforts should be made to reach high-risk groups, which include, in addition to commercial sex workers, the men who hire them, truck drivers, and migrant laborers. Projects in Peru, Tanzania, Thailand, and Zimbabwe have successfully persuaded prostitutes and their clients to use condoms more regularly. Thailand's program of 100 percent condom use in brothels now covers sixty-six of the country's seventy-three provinces (Rojanapithayakorn 1992).

■ *Diagnosis and treatment for a broader range of RTIs.* Efforts should be expanded to all women of reproductive age and should cover a broader range of RTIs, particularly pelvic inflammatory disease and some genital ulcers. Although treating patients with symptoms can help to avert serious complications and the further spread of STDs, the majority of women with STDs are asymptomatic. Furthermore, diagnosis of syndromes, such as abnormal vaginal discharge, requires the use of algorithms and/or simple diagnostic tests. Therefore, in settings where diagnostic facilities exist, specific diagnosis and appropriate treatment should be made available to women with symptoms suggestive of STDs and to asymptomatic women, especially those considered at risk, who attend prenatal, family planning, or primary health care facilities.

■ *Partner notification.* By placing increased emphasis on notifying the partner of a person diagnosed with an STD, health workers can reduce the spread of such diseases, including HIV/AIDS, and prevent reinfection after treatment. Because men more frequently have symptoms, they may be more likely than women to seek care. Partner notification can lead to earlier treatment for women, thereby reducing the rate of serious complications.

BOX 3.3 INAPPROPRIATE PRACTICES IN WOMEN'S HEALTH CARE

When misapplied, some health care practices can jeopardize the health of the women they are intended to benefit, as well as squander valuable health sector resources.

Misplaced emphasis in prenatal care. Appropriate prenatal care with backup for managing obstetric complications is essential for maternal and child health. Many countries, however, emphasize the number of prenatal visits, rather than the quality of care provided. Encouraging frequent visits strains the resources of both the patient (who incurs travel and time costs) and the health system. Prenatal care is often overly dominated by an ineffective effort to predict pregnancy complications, most of which are unpredictable.

In the former Soviet republics, women are seen at least twelve times (and often more than twenty) during pregnancy, and prenatal visits are marked by numerous diagnostic and lab tests, including routine ultrasonography. Little counseling and education regarding nutrition and family planning is provided (Weinstein, Oliveras, and MacIntosh 1993). When properly conducted, good-quality prenatal care can be provided through as few as three to six prenatal visits.

Unwarranted cesarean sections. Under appropriate conditions, cesarean section can be a lifesaving procedure for the mother and infant. However, the incidence of cesarean sections is not always justified on medical grounds. In Brazil, for example, the cesarean rate exceeds 30 percent (PAHO 1993). By contrast, cesarean rates range from 5 to 20 percent in industrial countries (Chalmers, Enkin, and Kierse 1989.) Misuse of cesarean sections not only adds to health care costs (raising costs by $13.4 million in Brazil in 1985) but also exposes women to far greater health risks than they face during vaginal deliveries. Studies in Latin America indicate that the decision to perform cesarean sections is based not only on maternal or fetal need but also on economic considerations of health care providers and hospitals (PAHO 1993) and the convenience of both the provider and patient.

Misdirected screening for cervical cancer. The limited cervical cancer screening conducted in developing countries is generally provided through family planning and maternal and child health clinics. Such an approach erroneously targets younger women rather than those aged 35 years or older, who are most at risk in most regions. Screening women from age 35 has been shown to be at least 90 percent as effective as screening from age 25 and to cut costs by one-third (Miller 1992).

■ *Reducing the transmission of HIV through blood transfusions.* Pregnant women, in particular, have an increased exposure to blood transfusions. Educating health care providers about possible risks and establishing guidelines can reduce the number of transfusions by more than 50 percent at negligible expense (World Bank 1993b). Where blood banks exist, donated blood can be screened for an additional cost of about 5 percent. Where such facilities are not available, rapid tests (such as the dipstick) are needed.

■ *HIV counseling and testing.* Where HIV prevalence is high, women of reproductive age should receive counseling and have the option of being tested for the virus. HIV-infected pregnant women should be counseled about the risk that their child may be HIV-infected, and they should be informed of their options. These may include abortion and, where affordable, therapy with AZT, a drug that may reduce risk of transmission to newborns by as much as two-thirds (CDC 1994).

Nutrition assistance for vulnerable groups.   The essential services focus on nutrition assistance for pregnant women. Expanded services should extend this assistance to other groups at risk of malnutrition, including young girls, adolescent girls, and elderly women. Special programs for refugees and dislocated persons may also be needed.

Nutrition strategies fall into two major categories: (a) decreasing energy loss by controlling fertility, preventing infections, and reducing the physical workload, and (b) increasing intake by improving the diet, reducing inhibitors that limit the efficiency of food absorption, and providing food and micronutrient supplements. Nutrition programs should assess the nutritional status of girls and women at risk and provide food supplements as needed, improve nutritional habits through counseling and public education, and identify appropriate local food sources. In collaboration with other agencies, nutrition programs should promote healthier fertility patterns and greater use of labor-saving technologies (Ghassemi 1990).

Governments can promote better nutrition by ensuring that low-income families have the means to purchase nutritious foods. Measures to ensure adequate food supplies include consumer price supports for staple foods, income transfers for vulnerable households, and food fortification.

Three major types of nutrition interventions can be used to improve the nutritional status of women and girls.

■ *Food supplementation.* If properly targeted and tailored to local market conditions, food supplementation programs can have a substantial impact on nutritional status (World Bank 1993b). In Guatemala, for instance, pregnant women who received food supplements had babies with higher birthweights than women who received no supplements (Villar and Rivera 1988). Although food supplementation programs are costly to implement and maintain, they may be the only effective means of improving the nutritional status of extremely poor populations.

■ *Micronutrient supplementation.* Appropriate micronutrient supplementation throughout the life cycle—such as iron and folate pills, vitamin A capsules, and iodized oil—can be highly effective in overcoming related deficiencies (World Bank 1993b). Most micronutrient programs cost less than $50 per DALY gained (for more details, see World Bank forthcoming).

■ *Food fortification.* Adding micronutrients (such as iron, vitamin A, and iodine) to processed foods can be a simpler and quicker means of improving nutritional status than changing diets. To be effective, fortified foods must be readily available, widely consumed by the target population, and relatively inexpensive (World Bank 1993b). Food fortification is a cost-effective option where adequate infrastructure is in place.

Screening, treatment, and referral for victims of violence. Health care providers can play a key role in identifying survivors of violence and referring them to appropriate social and legal services. Only a few simple questions are needed to screen for physical or sexual abuse. Screening programs can be introduced in prenatal clinics, emergency rooms, and other health facilities to assess women's risk of exposure to violence. Health facility protocols designed to identify victims of violence can help ensure timely intervention and gather information on the severity of the problem. Health care providers and other professionals who deal with women need to be trained to recognize signs of abuse, record information on the incidence and consequences of violence, provide sensitive counseling and treatment, collect legal evidence for the prosecution, and refer victims to appropriate services.

At least forty developing countries have NGOs that assist survivors of violence through rape crisis centers, centers for battered women, legal aid, and other services. A few governments, including those of Brazil, Mexico, and Papua New Guinea, also provide services to battered women and rape victims. Malaysia has formed women-only teams at police stations and hospitals. In Costa Rica one NGO trains teachers, therapists, and social workers to run support groups for victims of sexual abuse (Heise, Pitanguy, and Germain 1994).

Specific violence-related services that health agencies should offer are:

■ *Postcoital contraception for rape victims.* Offering postcoital pills, IUD insertion, or abortion to rape victims can spare them the additional trauma of unwanted pregnancy.

■ *Screening and referral.* Health care workers can perform an important service simply by breaching the wall of silence that surrounds abuse and putting women in contact with services designed to deal with violence-related problems. Screening should be conducted privately and be as noninvasive as possible, as part of a more general process of questioning about the woman's sexual and gynecological history. Clinic staff should contact local women's groups to familiarize themselves with support services. Often, advocacy groups and crisis centers have information materials that can be displayed in waiting areas.

■ *Record keeping.* To interrupt the cycle of violence, health care providers need to take special care to collect evidence of violence in a form that is adequate for legal action. Such information can also be used to document the extent of violence.

Cancer Screening and Treatment

Early detection of cancer is important because treatment is most effective in the early stages of the disease. The cost-effectiveness of cancer-screening programs depends on the incidence of the disease, the technical feasibility of screening and treatment at early stages, and the possibility of targeting high-risk groups.

Cervical cancer.   Screening for cervical cancer is particularly cost-effective because the disease can be treated relatively easily in its early stages. The most common screening method is the Pap smear, but other, more economical, methods (such as visual examination, either unaided or aided by low-power magnification, and acetic acid treatment of the cervix) are now being evaluated for clinical use. Treatment of preinvasive cervical lesions is very successful and can be conducted cost-effectively using cryotherapy and loop excision. Treatment for more advanced stages requires surgery and sometimes radiation, which are far less effective and more expensive (Miller 1992).

Studies have shown that screening all women once in their lifetime prevents many more cases of cervical cancer than screening a small proportion of women every few years. The goal should be to screen every woman 35 to 40 years of age at least once. If more resources are available, the frequency of screening could be increased to every ten years for women aged 35 to 55. If a high proportion of the target group is being screened, and resources permit, screening should be extended first to older women up to age 60 and then to younger women down to age 25 (Miller 1992; see also Box 3.3). In parts of Africa, cervical cancer appears to occur earlier than in other countries, and thus targeting women younger than 35 before targeting those over 55 may be more cost-effective.

A program that screens all women over age 35 for cervical cancer at five-year intervals costs an average of $100 per DALY gained. Increasing the screening interval reduces the cost (Jamison 1993). In countries where resources are more limited, feasible and cost-effective screening programs should treat only severe dysplasia or carcinoma in situ and should use such relatively inexpensive outpatient treatments as cryotherapy and loop excision (Sherris and others 1993).

Breast cancer.   Early detection is equally important for breast cancer. The most cost-effective method of breast cancer screening is physical examination (both by the woman herself and by health care providers). Physical examination alone can detect about two-thirds of the cancers detected by mammography. Where additional resources are available and breast cancer is common, mammography can be used as a diagnostic tool, although this increases the cost tenfold when done on an annual basis. Screening programs that include periodic examination by a trained health worker and a mammogram once a year for women aged 50 to 69 can reduce breast cancer mortality by 30 to 40 percent when appropriate treatment is provided (Miller and others 1990). Treatment of breast cancer, however, requires relatively expensive surgery, radiation therapy, and chemotherapy and is not likely to be cost-effective in many developing-country settings.

The inclusion of breast cancer management in the expanded services will depend on local prevalence and resource availability. In countries where the incidence of breast cancer is on the rise (because of declining fertility, dietary influences, and environmental carcinogens) and where adequate resources are available, breast cancer screening and treatment may form a component of the expanded services.

Expanded Interventions for Behavioral Change

Most health services have paid little attention to the special health needs of school-age girls and adolescents, which differ from those of young children and adults. Adolescence, in particular, is a period of rapid change and growth. Overall health status during these years carries over into adulthood. It is also the time when unhealthy behaviors may begin.

Health services could realize substantial benefits by intensifying programs for school-age girls and especially adolescents. Programs need to appeal to these young women directly by focusing on their needs and preferences. In general, reaching them through existing institutions, such as schools, is more cost-effective than motivating them to come to a new site. Since peer education programs have been more effective than adult-directed initiatives, youths should be involved in program planning and implementation.

Health Education for Early Prevention of Health Problems

Working through education systems, governments can provide information to girls and adolescents on general health and disease prevention, contraception, STDs, HIV/AIDS, substance abuse, and nutritional needs. School curricula can also cover communication skills, strategies for resisting peer pressure, and negotiating techniques. A curriculum on "Life Planning" that emphasizes experiential, interactive learning and puts sexuality in a broader life context has proved successful in increasing knowledge and changing attitudes (WHO 1992a). Governments can also support nonformal education programs, including peer education and community outreach, in order to reach adolescents where they live, learn, work, and play.

With the AIDS pandemic making early sexual experimentation potentially life-threatening, it is particularly vital that preteen and adolescent girls understand the basic facts about sexuality and reproductive health so that they can make responsible decisions about their sexual behavior. Sex education and contraceptive services must be made available in all cultural settings, regardless of age or marital status. Restricting adolescents' access to contraceptive information and services has not reduced premarital sexual activity, but it has left adolescents without the means to make responsible choices and protect themselves from unintended pregnancy, STDs, and HIV.

Young people and their caregivers are often unaware of the increased need for energy-producing foods and micronutrients during adolescence to support physical development and prepare young women for childbearing. Nutrition education, provided through multiservice and vocational training centers, has been effective in improving adolescents' nutritional status (WHO 1986).

In all countries adolescence is a period when important lifestyle patterns are established, making it an important time to influence decisions about the use of tobacco, alcohol, and drugs. Since smoking is increasing fastest among young women, public education programs, school curricula, and advertising regulations can place special emphasis on persuading young women not to smoke. Mass media campaigns can counter advertising directed to young women that portrays smoking as glamorous and sophisticated behavior. Governments can also restrict the advertising and sale of tobacco products to minors, tax such products, and regulate tobacco production and imports. Messages need to stress the hazards and disadvantages of smoking and to promote alternative strategies for coping with stress.

Increased Efforts to Reduce Gender Discrimination and Violence

Instead of merely treating injuries, malnutrition, and other health problems that derive from society's general neglect of women, governments can move vigorously to address gender discrimination and violence. Countries that can afford to go beyond the essential services should define clear strategies for reducing discriminatory attitudes and practices and gender-related violence.

Health agencies should concentrate on three major areas:

■ *Public education initiatives.* Much can be accomplished by bringing attention to the social practices that favor males and perpetuate violence against women and by emphasizing the harmful effects of such practices on women's health. Public education initiatives can influence the content of popular radio and television programs, educate media representatives, and promote news coverage of gender discrimination and violence.

■ *Health care training.* Regular pre- and in-service training for health care providers is needed to sensitize staff to practices that are harmful to women and to teach the skills needed to address these practices. Health care providers need to be aware of possible barriers to communication with female clients and of ways to elicit women's judgments about their own health needs and to meet these needs effectively.

■ *Community participation.* Although health care providers can deal with only a fraction of the problems associated with discrimination and violence against women, they can put women in touch with other support agencies. To do this, they need to establish ties with law, education, employment, credit, and community resources and to support networks of professionals and community activists.

Women beyond Reproductive Age

To improve the health and productivity of women aged 45 and older, as well as the associated costs of curative care, more attention needs to be given to preventing problems—through proper diet and exercise; avoidance of tobacco, excessive alcohol, and other harmful substances; screening for cervical cancer and other chronic diseases to the extent that resources permit; and health education to promote self-help.

Health care providers should advise women of all ages of the importance of an adequate diet. Osteoporosis, for instance, which accelerates after menopause, is best prevented through early intake of sufficient levels of calcium. To reduce the risk of bone fracture after menopause, women should be encouraged to improve their diet, exercise regularly, stop smoking, and reduce their consumption of alcohol. Although estrogen therapy is known to retard bone loss, it is not yet a cost-effective public health measure for developing countries (Lindsay 1993).

As women approach menopause (generally between ages 45 and 55), they need counseling about the physical and mental symptoms that may develop as their estrogen levels decline. For most women these symptoms are relatively mild and subside within two years. In counseling menopausal women and helping them to cope with hormonal changes, health care providers should be instructed to be reassuring and compassionate.

With increasing widowhood and divorce, and changing household composition, an increasing number of households are headed by women who may need assistance to meet their domestic, childrearing, and economic responsibilities. Many older women now live alone, which contributes to their isolation and can make it difficult for them to eat properly and maintain their health. In some places widows are subject to active discrimination, exacerbated by inheritance laws and customs that fail to protect their rights.

Sustainable solutions will need to rely on efforts to integrate older women into the community and increase their capacity for self-help. Health care providers can relieve the isolation of elderly women and improve their medical and social condition by linking them with support networks such as day centers for the elderly, peer groups, and agencies that provide food and housing. For cxample, the Center of the Aged in India promotes community-based services such as drop-in facilities for seniors, often run by the elderly themselves (Tout 1989).

CHAPTER FOUR

Issues for National Program Planning

Bringing about real change in women's health requires strong government commitment, a favorable policy environment, and adequate resources. Much can be accomplished by redirecting public financing away from tertiary (specialized) hospitals, specialist training, and less cost-effective curative care to the highly cost-effective packages of essential and expanded services (Chapter 3) and by delivering services more efficiently. Involving women in planning and design makes service delivery more responsive to women's needs and improves utilization and impact.

Policymakers should foster cooperation with the private sector—including NGOs—to maximize resources and extend care to women not reached by government programs. Some countries have established an office in the ministry of health to develop and monitor a women's health policy and action plan, in coordination both with other parts of the government that are focusing on women and with representatives of women's groups. Finally, governments should routinely collect and analyze gender-specific health data as a basis for policymaking, resource allocation, and program design and evaluation.

This chapter discusses the actions that governments can take immediately to improve women's health: broadening policy support; adopting supportive legislation, policies, and regulatory mechanisms; improving financing; strengthening the delivery, coverage, and quality of health care services; promoting women's involvement in planning and implementing health programs; collaborating with NGOs and private sector providers; expanding health education; and undertaking research and evaluation.

Broadening Policy Support

Governments can use legal and regulatory mechanisms to support improvements in women's health and nutrition that can have far-reaching effects. A health-oriented policy agenda beneficial to women should call for the following actions.

■ *Invest more in female education.* Women who are better educated take better care of their own health and that of their children. All girls, including those who become pregnant, should be encouraged and given equal opportunity to attend school.

■ *Strengthen legislative and other support for women's nutrition.* Four policy initiatives can help improve women's nutritional status: fortification of foods with iodine and iron; consumer food subsidies and targeted food distribution; dissemination of labor-saving devices for women; and better access for women to agricultural extension services and credit.

■ *Reduce discrimination against females.* Discriminatory policies affect women's health by restricting their ability to adopt healthy behaviors and by limiting their opportunities for economic advancement. Examples of such policies include employment practices that handicap women, limits on women's control over family resources, restrictions on women's ability to travel or obtain credit, and laws permitting early marriage for women. In most countries, for example, the legal age of marriage is at least two years lower for women than for men.

■ *Abolish practices harmful to women's health.* Through legislation, legal enforcement, and public education programs, governments have the power to curb practices that harm women or are injurious to their health. For example, governments can ban female genital mutilation or lend their authority to campaigns to change public attitudes and behavior. They can tax tobacco products and other harmful substances, restrict their sale, and regulate their advertising. By enacting and enforcing criminal penalties for violence against women, governments can deter such crimes.

■ *Remove legal impediments to the effective delivery of health services.* Governments can change laws and regulations that restrict women's access to essential health services. Examples are restrictions on legal access to contraception and pregnancy termination; barriers to service use based on age, marital status, or other factors; spousal consent requirements; and import duties on contraceptives and drugs. States that ratify the 1979 Convention on the Elimination of All Forms of Discrimination against Women pledge to eliminate discrimination in health care and family planning, among other areas.

■ *Support appropriate training and increased responsibility for nurses and midwives.* Women's access to health services can be improved by removing legislative and licensing obstacles for health care providers other than physicians. Nurses and midwives could provide most of the essential and expanded services for women. Success in modifying current practices, however, will require the support of professional associations representing physicians and other health practitioners.

■ *Encourage private sector participation.* Governments can offer subsidies, tax incentives, loans, clinic space, equipment, free publicity, and other benefits to private sector providers to encourage them to better meet women's health care needs. To ensure that private providers offer high-quality services, governments can establish and monitor performance standards, enforced through licensing exams and periodic reexaminations of health professionals; accredit health worker training programs; and inspect facilities.

Improving the Equity and Efficiency of Health Financing

One of the most difficult health policy issues is deciding how to allocate public resources to achieve the greatest impact on overall health status. *World Development Report 1993* (World Bank 1993b) argues that governments can develop a national package of highly cost-effective public health interventions and essential clinical services, which, if broadly extended to the population, could substantially reduce disease. Any national health package that is designed to maximize cost-effectiveness and reduce the disease burden will necessarily give considerable weight to health interventions for women, because, as discussed in Chapter 3, many such interventions produce large health gains relative to their costs. Within this framework, the essential services for women identified in this book would represent a subset of the national health package.

Selecting Interventions for Public Financing

The criteria for selecting and financing the essential services for women parallel those presented in *World Development Report 1993* for the broader national health package (see Box 1.1). The most cost-effective interventions are selected for inclusion in the package, provided they also address a substantial share of the disease burden in a given country. As more resources become available, permitting a more comprehensive package, the next most cost-effective interventions are added.

There is a strong argument for publicly funding the public health interventions in the package of essential services for women because of their nature as public goods—one individual can use or benefit from them without limiting others' consumption or benefit. The private sector will not supply public goods because it cannot easily charge for them. Public financing is also easily justified for some clinical services because of their large positive spillover effects, or externalities: averting or treating an STD, for example, benefits not only the woman treated but others in society (including her offspring) who might later have contracted the disease. Also, fairness and equity argue strongly for the provision of free or highly subsidized essential services to poor women. Services for more advantaged groups can be financed out-of-pocket or through insurance.

Not surprisingly, there is a tradeoff between the population covered and the comprehensiveness of health services that are publicly financed. As argued in *World Development Report 1993*, the more narrowly that interventions can be targeted just to the poor, the more comprehensive the services in the package can afford to be.

Not all the health services that are publicly funded need to be provided by the state. Governments can finance maternity care for poor women through private providers and NGOs, for example. Whether or not it provides the services itself, however, the government has a key role to play in providing policy direction and guidance, promoting efficient and cost-effective approaches, and facilitating private participation in the delivery of services.

Cost Recovery and Targeting Public Expenditures to the Poor

In countries with severe constraints on public funds for health care, user fees may have to be charged to help support the essential services for women and the rest of the national package. Within an appropriately designed price structure, user fees can encourage the efficient use of referral systems and stretch scarce public funds. Overall, health system costs can be reduced—for example, by having paramedics provide free services at local health centers while charging for the same services in hospitals, thereby reserving specialized care for complicated cases. Modest user fees that are rolled over to improve service quality can even increase the use of services by the poor (Litvack and Bodart 1993). User fees can also be used to fully recover costs from services outside the national package. Everything beyond the essential or expanded national package is discretionary and could be financed from private sources (through insurance or out-of-pocket payments by users).

In designing user fees, it is important to incorporate mechanisms to protect the poor. The practical use of any targeting mechanism will depend on its impact on demand, its administrative costs, its technical and managerial requirements, and the level of political support. Poor individuals, identified on the basis of income or nutritional status, can be provided with the essential services free or on a sliding scale. Vouchers can be provided to give the poor a broader choice of providers. Subsidized essential services can also be targeted to easily identifiable subgroups of the population, such as the residents of a poor neighborhood. Self-targeting is applicable if services have characteristics that imply that only the poor tend to use them (time costs or fewer amenities, for example). These same characteristics, however, may also deter much of the poor population from using services. Finally, public expenditures can be targeted by type of service. If STDs are more prevalent among the poor, then free or highly subsidized STD services would disproportionately benefit the poor.

Any user fees imposed on the poor would have to be very low, and demand for services should be monitored to ensure that the fees do not restrict access to care. User fees may constitute a severe impediment to low-income women with limited resources and weak claims on household resources. When user fees were introduced for some services at the Ahmadu Bello University Hospital in Zaria, Nigeria, in 1985, the number of obstetric admissions fell. Admissions dropped even further when additional charges were levied in 1988, and maternal mortality rose in the hospital's catchment area (Ekwempu and others 1990). Similarly, the number of women attending a public outpatient clinic for STDs in Nairobi plummeted by 65 percent after user fees were imposed; male attendance decreased by 40 percent (Moses and others 1992).

Strengthening Service Delivery

Governments can influence the coverage and quality of health services through attention to the following areas: access to services; delivery strategies; infrastructure; quality of care; number and distribution of female health care providers; and responsibilities of nonphysicians.

Increasing Women's Access to Care

Several key factors impede women's access to care.

- Adolescents' health needs are ignored and their sexuality is denied.
- Household decisionmakers may be unwilling to commit resources for women's health care, and women generally have less income and less control over family resources.
- Because of multiple roles in the workplace and at home, women often have difficulty getting away at the times when services are offered.

- Cultural norms and insufficient resources often make it difficult for women to travel to distant sites for medical care.
- Women often lack information about self-care and about when health care is needed or where it is available.
- Health providers may not have the basic training to provide the essential services for women and may be prohibited from practicing certain potentially lifesaving procedures.

To serve the greatest number of women, all essential services should be made available at the most peripheral level of care appropriate (for example, at home or at a local health center). Health care at the community level, backed up by referral facilities, is especially important for women, particularly in the reproductive years. Incentives to encourage health care providers to work in remote communities can increase access to services.

Designing Delivery Strategies to Meet Women's Needs

Outreach programs can extend the reach of services to girls and women and ensure that referrals to higher-level centers are made as needed. Through home visits to parents who neglected to take their underweight children to a feeding center, for example, a Punjabi child health and nutrition project reduced mortality rates 11 percent for girls under age 5 in twenty-six rural villages. Because workers from the center supervised the feeding, they were able to redress a food allocation system that favors boys (Pebley and Amin 1991). Where women's travel is severely restricted (as in some Muslim countries), outreach and community-based services are especially important. Mobile clinics can also bring services closer to women.

Clustering services for women and children (such as family planning, postpartum care, and well-baby care) at the same place and time often promotes positive interactions in health benefits and reduces service delivery costs and women's time and travel costs (Leslie 1992). In Ethiopia, utilization rose substantially following the integration of curative care, growth monitoring, vaccination, prenatal care, and family planning services (Walley, Tefera, and McDonald 1991). Programs also need to address constraints on girls and women's time. In a supplemental food program in India, women were found to be more likely to participate if food rations were prepared in advance and women could pick them up on the way to the fields (King and others 1986).

Integrating services requires some vigilance, however, to avoid overburdening health care providers, planners, and supervisors or downplaying women's health services. In integrated maternal and child health programs over the past three decades, for example, maternity care was overshadowed by child survival strategies. Also, the more varied the range of services, the greater the need for training and technical resources.

In some contexts, separate services for women may be appropriate. Adolescent girls, in particular, are not likely to use general maternal and child health services and may prefer facilities that are specially designed to offer young people sympathetic, nonjudgmental counseling. Women may prefer a separate, private setting for fertility regulation. Because of women's limited financial resources and time and their varying needs, it is important that health care delivery points be conveniently located and provide as much choice as possible in specialized and integrated services.

Strengthening the Health Care Delivery Infrastructure

To improve women's health, governments will often need to shift resources from centralized, tertiary-care facilities to health services at the district level. Additional resources may be required to improve health facility infrastructure, to finance vehicles and communication systems for referrals, to expand training for primary health care providers, and to set up reliable and efficient supply systems.

Health workers at all levels require basic equipment and supplies (including contraceptives, iron and folate tablets, safe-birth kits, diagnostics for STDs, and antibiotics). A World Bank sectoral study in India found that a program to reduce anemia among high-risk women failed because only 12 percent of the intended beneficiaries were offered iron and folate tablets, and almost 80 percent of these women dropped out because of a shortage of tablets.

Improving the Quality of Services for Women

Even where health services are readily available and affordable, women may not use them if their quality is poor (Parker and others 1990; Simmons, Koenig, and Huque 1990; CIAES 1991). Studies have found that quality of care is a significant factor in a woman's decision to seek prenatal care (Parker and others 1990; Locay, Sanderson, and Weeks 1990; CIAES 1991), to give birth at a clinic instead of at home (Sargent 1989), or to continue using contraception (Mensch 1993).

Poor-quality services generally result from a lack of infrastructure, insufficient staffing or high absenteeism, lack of female health care providers, inadequate training, insensitivity to patients, shortages of equipment and supplies, and inadequate monitoring and supervision. Inconvenient hours, limited services, long waits, lack of privacy or confidentiality, and overcrowded waiting rooms all reflect poorly on service quality and standards.

There are several key initiatives governments can take to improve the quality of women's health services.

■ *Strengthening provider competence.* Training curricula and supervisory systems should cover topics related to women's particular health care needs. Health care workers may have to acquire new technical skills, such as the use of the partograph in labor or manual vacuum aspiration, to manage pregnancy complications and make appropriate referrals. Physicians, midwives, nurses, and community-level workers need an understanding of gender issues and the social, cultural, and psychological aspects of sexuality and reproduction. Good communication skills are also important.

■ *Educating patients.* Because women are often unfamiliar with preventive measures and treatment alternatives, health care providers need to provide full information and counseling on these issues to help women assess their own health care needs (Bruce 1990).

■ *Offering continuity of care.* Programs should include mechanisms to ensure continuity of care and follow-up, especially for family planning, prenatal and postpartum care, and the prevention and treatment of STDs. Good provider-client relations are critical to effective follow-up, since patients are most apt to heed the advice of health care providers they know and trust. In addition, procedures are necessary for recording patient history, setting follow-up appointments, scheduling home visits or other outreach services, and ensuring referral to other facilities.

■ *Protecting privacy.* Health care providers should ensure that women can speak with them in confidence and that physical examinations are performed with appropriate respect for privacy.

Increasing the Number of Female Health Care Providers

Some cultures discourage women from consulting male health care providers. In Egypt, for example, most trained health care workers are male, and women often avoid seeking treatment (Krieger and ElFeraly 1991). In such cases, increasing the number of female health workers could improve service quality and use (Chatterjee and Lambert 1989). In some settings, however, similar barriers prevent female providers from working in remote areas. In recognition of this problem, the Aga Khan Development Network in Pakistan has trained women to work in their own communities as lady health visitors.

Female health care providers can play an important role in educating women to recognize their health and nutrition needs. In Gujarat, India, women health workers from the SARTHI project offer individual and community support to victims of violence (Khanna 1992, cited in Heise, Pitanguy, and Germain 1994). In Longhus, China, female health professionals visit pregnant women in their homes to teach couples how to monitor delivery and recognize danger signs requiring treatment (Shen 1985, cited in APWRCN 1989).

In most developing countries, trained health care providers, particularly midwives and physicians, are concentrated in urban areas. Unsuitable accommodations in rural areas, cultural restrictions on women working in areas where they have no family, or the need to seek employment near their husbands all inhibit the rural deployment of female health care providers. Some francophone African countries guarantee women a position near that of their husbands, with the result that a disproportionate number of midwives are assigned to urban hospitals. Some countries have addressed this problem by requiring all newly qualified physicians and nurses to serve in rural areas (WHO 1991b) and by encouraging local communities to provide free housing for health care providers.

Delegating Responsibility to Nonphysicians

Many countries have laws and practices that make it difficult for health care providers who are not physicians—particularly midwives—to administer certain essential women's health services. In many parts of the world, midwives cannot legally use vacuum extractors or forceps for delivery, give oxytocic drugs without a physician's order, or prescribe antibiotics. Midwives need to be trained so that they are capable of providing independent care, particularly in rural areas. In Zaire, women's lives have been saved by allowing nurses, who are more readily available than physicians during births, to perform cesarean sections (White, Thorpe, and Maine 1987).

The shortage of physicians (especially women physicians) in some developing countries is well recognized. Less attention has been given to the shortage of trained nurses and midwives, which may be worsening in some areas. A trained nurse-midwife must be able not only to deliver babies and care for newborns, but also to give the necessary supervision, care, and advice to women during pregnancy, labor, and the postpartum period (WHO 1993a). WHO estimates that one midwife can handle about 200 deliveries a year; in a community with a crude birth rate of about 40 births per 1,000 population, therefore, one midwife would be needed for every 5,000 people (Kwast 1991). By these calculations, the number of midwives is seriously deficient in many countries

(Kwast 1993). All women should have reasonable access—within two hours, wherever possible—to a health center with a nurse-midwife.

Traditional birth attendants (TBAs) currently assist in about 60 to 80 percent of all births in developing countries (Leslie and Gupta 1989). Where reliance on TBAs is commonplace, superimposing a system of government-supported prenatal and delivery care is likely to be less effective than designing services to complement and strengthen existing patterns of care. A cadre of trained midwives could serve as the link between communities, TBAs, and the formal health care system.

Involving Women in Planning and Implementing Health Care Programs

The best way to ensure that service delivery strategies are designed with women's perspectives and needs in mind is to consult women about the approaches they prefer. Local women should be invited to serve on committees that advise on plans, procedures, and materials. The active involvement of program beneficiaries leads to increased use of services. In Peru contraceptive use jumped by more than 50 percent in the project zone after the women's organization Peru-Mujer engaged low-income women in the design of educational materials on family planning (Figueroa 1992). Bringing female health care providers into leadership positions in the health sector—not only in traditional women's roles but in management, planning, implementation, and research as well—will also help to improve women's health programs.

Strengthening Collaboration with the Private Sector

To achieve widespread and efficient coverage of the essential services, governments will have an interest in encouraging a private sector role in financing and service provision. Numerous NGOs, financed publicly or privately, provide health and nutrition services to women—often to poorer, difficult-to-reach groups—and are actively engaged in community development. In addition, for-profit private sector providers can complement government health services by providing the essential services to those who can afford them and offering a broader array of health care options.

Nongovernmental Organizations

Governments can assist NGOs to provide women's health and nutrition services by simplifying registration procedures, providing tax incentives and subsidies, and offering training, office space, and supplies. Involving NGOs in program planning, implementation, and evaluation often benefits government programs as well.

Certain characteristics of NGOs may make them particularly well suited to reaching underserved or disadvantaged populations, such as refugee groups, more successfully than government services. Known in the community, they are able to test and adapt new approaches to health care delivery and can complement and enhance government services. They can also work in areas considered too controversial for government intervention.

NGOs can be effective agents of change by challenging existing services and delivery mechanisms and by pressuring decisionmakers to meet women's health needs. Many women's groups, even those that are not involved in delivering health and nutrition services, can play a key role in making women aware of the health services that are available and encouraging their use. They can also serve as a source of information to health program planners about women's priorities and the constraints they face in improving their health. In particular, NGOs can promote intersectoral collaboration in efforts to improve adolescent health and to reduce violence against women.

The following examples illustrate the range of NGO involvement in women's health activities.

■ The Bangladesh Women's Health Coalition, which began as an urban clinic offering menstrual regulation services, provides a wide range of reproductive health services to approximately 97,000 women and children in urban and rural areas. Its experience demonstrates that integrated services and improved care (for example, treating clients with respect and ensuring privacy) can increase effective use of services at less cost than standard family planning clinics (Kay, Germain, and Bangser 1991).

■ The National Association of Nigerian Nurses and Midwives developed a communication program to advocate the eradication of female genital mutilation. Nurses and midwives discussed the harmful effects of female genital mutilation during talks in clinics and included it as a topic in nursing and medical school curricula. In one state the association introduced a symbolic dress to replace the scarring that traditionally marked the passage into womanhood (Adebajo and others 1990).

■ The Cairo Women's Health Book Collective has published the only book of practical health information for women available in Arabic (Ibrahim and Farah 1992).

For-Profit Providers

Governments can encourage private providers to expand and improve services for women's health by mandating the inclusion of essential services for women in insurance policies and by providing subsidies to ensure the provision of these services to low-income women. Insurance schemes that cover prenatal and delivery care, for instance, are useful in expanding women's health care. In 1984 the Mexican Social Security Institute, financed mainly by employers, spent nearly $40 million on family planning services in urban areas—an investment that saved about $210 million in maternity care costs, $10 million in treatment of incomplete abortions, and $130 million in health care for infants (Nortman and Halvas 1986).

To expand access to health products that require little or no medical intervention (such as certain contraceptives, vitamins, malaria drugs and bed nets, treatment kits for STDs, iron and folate tablets, and fortified foods), governments can encourage sales through commercial outlets. Small shops, pharmacies, markets, and street stalls that are conveniently located are an underused resource for bringing health care to women and reducing related travel and time costs. Pharmacies in developing countries now serve about 15 million contraceptive users and could potentially reach 85 million couples who can afford contraceptives (Lande and Blackburn 1989).

Intensifying Public Education

Public education programs can be used to advocate new policies, promote services and positive health practices, and get feedback from patients to improve the quality of care.

Promoting Health Services and Healthy Behaviors

Women and other family decisionmakers need to understand the importance of preventive services, maternity care, and good nutrition. Broad public education programs are needed to promote women's health services and healthy behaviors. Public education programs can also help women locate appropriate health services and can convey information about clinic hours, costs, and requirements for access. In areas where husbands, relatives, and community members are the principal decisionmakers on women's access to health care, these groups should be targeted to receive related messages.

Advocacy for Policy Change

Advocacy programs are designed to increase awareness of women's health problems among policymakers (political, medical, media, and religious), to create a policy environment favorable to health reform both within and beyond the health sector, and to lobby for improved women's health services. For example, the national women's commission in Chile has adopted an extensive program to promote the criminalization of domestic violence, document the dimensions of this problem, organize community awareness campaigns, and establish crisis centers that provide legal and psychological support (Servicio Nacional de la Mujer 1991).

Behavioral Change

The first step in influencing health-related behaviors is often to increase awareness of conditions that put women at risk. For example, most women and their families are not aware of the warning signs of pregnancy-related complications and so do not respond properly to them. Even violence against women may be viewed as normal and not a cause for seeking assistance. Public education programs can promote actions in the home or community to improve women's health and prevent future health problems. Public education programs can also discourage unsafe practices that harm women's health (such as female genital mutilation, risky sexual behavior, inadequate food consumption during pregnancy, unsafe delivery practices, and smoking). Information needs to target not only women but also their parents, husbands, in-laws, and village leaders. Husbands, in particular, have a major impact on women's workload, diet, exposure to STDs, and use of health services and contraception.

The mass media now reach vast audiences in developing countries and have enormous potential to communicate information along with new values and ideas. Mass media campaigns have been used for family planning, nutrition, breastfeeding promotion, and AIDS prevention. Songs, radio programs, and films have been especially effective in informing adolescents about responsible sexual behavior and pregnancy. A study in Latin America found that two popular songs promoting abstinence influenced teenage girls to discuss sexuality issues with their parents and others (PCS 1992).

Because women have lower literacy levels than men and may have less access to mass media, personal sources of information, such as friends, relatives, teachers, outreach workers, and community leaders, remain important for behavioral change. Public education programs need to ensure that mass media messages are reinforced by health care providers to reach women directly.

Meeting Information Needs

A major constraint to improving women's health services has been a lack of information on the causes, severity, and distribution of women's health and nutrition problems, as well as on the relative effectiveness and cost of interventions. Research, monitoring, and evaluation are integral to program development and service delivery; inadequate information leads to ineffective programs and wasted resources.

Health Status Indicators

Biomedical, epidemiological, and socioeconomic data are needed to assess women's health status and evaluate related interventions. Such data are often unavailable or of poor quality. In particular, many developing countries lack a complete and accurate vital registration system. Even where vital registration systems exist, the cause of death is often incorrectly reported or omitted altogether. Maternal mortality is often underreported, due to a variety of social, religious, emotional, and practical factors, such as the stigma of abortion, the desire to avoid an official inquiry into the cause of death, and the failure to indicate pregnancy as the precipitating cause of death (WHO 1991a).

Governments should insist that health and nutrition data be disaggregated by gender as well as age group. Breaking down data for age groups of five years or less provides a clearer picture of the needs of key groups such as adolescents. Population-based studies and data on morbidity are especially needed (ICRW 1989). Data on women's life circumstances and needs would promote better understanding of the social, cultural, legal, economic, and psychological factors that affect women's ability to protect their own health.

Some health problems affecting women—those related to abortion, adolescent pregnancy, female genital mutilation, and domestic violence—are controversial and difficult to document. Even in industrial countries, their incidence and consequences often go unreported or are misclassified. But where health care providers are alerted to problems such as domestic violence, women do report abuse (Heise, Pitanguy, and Germain 1994). Still other problems (such as maternal mortality) are difficult to measure because their relative infrequency makes it necessary to study large populations at substantial expense.

Given the paucity of data on women's health, health agencies should make full use of existing sources, including health facility data, patient records, vital statistics registration, population-based surveys, and continuous surveillance and monitoring systems. Sources outside the health sector (such as police records) may be needed for information on violence against women or substance abuse. Whenever possible, programs should rely on more efficient use of available data, supplemented by additional research as needed. Women's organizations and NGOs can be especially helpful in disseminating research findings.

Case histories, focus group discussions, in-depth interviews and observation, confidential inquiries, verbal autopsies, and death certificate reviews are also important sources of information on women's health. Qualitative research on intended beneficiaries and program personnel is especially important in designing programs for women. Program designers need to know women's priority concerns, the underlying causes (cultural, attitudinal, economic) of health problems, and the range of acceptable, affordable, and effective solutions. Local investigators, including women, should be involved in all aspects of related research.

Program Design

In many cases, available data are insufficient to plan and manage health programs, and agencies may need to conduct new studies to strengthen program design.

■ *Knowledge, attitude, and practice surveys.* Special studies can help provide insight into numerous issues, including the users' perspective and the local cultural and social context; the individual, social, and economic costs associated with the prevention and treatment of disease and injury; and providers' understanding of women's needs.

■ *Operations research.* Operations research can be used to test different approaches to service delivery and to identify and overcome program obstacles.

■ *Cost-effectiveness analysis.* Research on alternative approaches can help clarify choices regarding resource allocation.

Program Monitoring and Evaluation

Where data are available, health status indicators—changes in the prevalence of iron-deficiency anemia among pregnant women, for example, or in the proportion of deaths from obstructed labor or hemorrhage—can be used to measure program impact. Indicators should be developed in accordance with each country's resources, priorities, and needs. (A detailed list of indicators for measuring women's health status is provided by Tinker and others 1994 in *Women's Health and Nutrition: Making a Difference*). In many low-resource settings, data on program impact may be difficult and expensive to obtain, resulting in greater reliance on process indicators. Measuring the inputs and outputs of programs provides program managers with timely feedback on progress and affords an opportunity to adjust interventions and treatments as indicated. For example, the proportion of pregnant women who receive iron and folate tablets and counseling on the danger signs of pregnancy could indicate whether prenatal care services are adequate. A high proportion of appropriately treated obstetric complications would indicate an effective case detection, management, and referral system.

A major constraint on effective program monitoring and evaluation is the lack of an effective management information system in most developing countries. The system should integrate data collection and analysis into program operations and ensure that the results are provided to central and field-level managers to facilitate decisionmaking. Limiting the number of indicators to those integral to program operations can simplify data collection and analysis and ensure timely feedback.

Where monitoring systems are weak, alternative strategies can be introduced. In areas where home births are common, for example, periodic household interviews may be desirable. Some aspects of service quality can be inferred from process indicators such as the number of contraceptive methods available and the method mix among contraceptive users. Additional efforts are needed to assess other indicators of service quality (client waiting times, travel distances, and satisfaction with services received), since quality of care is a major factor affecting utilization. Direct observation of client-provider interactions, interviews with clients and staff, focus group discussions, and sample surveys can all be used to elicit information.

CHAPTER FIVE

Moving from Rhetoric
to Action

Sustainable improvement in the health systems of developing countries depends foremost on a nation's commitment to the health and well-being
of its people. Foreign assistance can play a critical role, however, by focusing
policy concern and ensuring that adequate resources are available. Foreign
assistance agencies can have an impact on women's health far beyond their
monetary contributions by making policymakers aware of the social and economic gains to be realized from lowering rates of female death and disability.
Perhaps most important, international agencies can help by sharing lessons
gleaned from other countries' experience and by supporting interventions that
have proven to be the most cost-effective.

World Bank Programs in Women's Health and Nutrition

World Bank lending for health, population, and nutrition has increased fivefold
over the past six years. Between 1986 and 1993 the World Bank allocated
nearly $5.7 billion to more than 100 health, population, and nutrition projects
with women's health components. These projects represent 90 percent of the
Bank's projects in this sector since 1986. Nearly half the projects with women's
health components are in Sub-Saharan Africa, one-fourth in Asia, and one-fifth
in Latin America. The following are the main areas in which the Bank has
supported activities since 1986.

■ *Safe motherhood*. In Indonesia the Bank is supporting the expansion of safe motherhood services to the village level. In Zimbabwe the Bank and other assistance agencies are collaborating to upgrade maternity care facilities, improve referral systems, and train nurse-midwives. In China the Bank funds training in maternal health care for female physicians and assists in making emergency obstetric services more accessible to poor women.

■ *Family planning*. A Bangladesh project supports family planning and maternal and child health services provided by female outreach workers. In Ukraine, where there are 1.5 abortions for every birth, the Bank is discussing a project with the ministry of health to strengthen maternal and child health services and provide contraceptive supplies to reduce women's reliance on abortion.

■ *STDs and AIDS*. In Lesotho the Bank is supporting prevention, diagnosis, and treatment of STDs and AIDS for women of reproductive age, as well as research on effective ways to extend services to commercial sex workers. Brazil's Bank-assisted National AIDS/STD Control Program includes mass media campaigns, education in the workplace, disease surveillance, and research.

■ *Adolescent sexuality*. The Bank has assisted the governments of Lesotho and Nigeria in developing school-based family life education programs and mass media campaigns to persuade adolescents to delay childbearing. Indonesia's population project includes clubs for young people and family planning messages on television, radio, and video aimed at youths.

■ *Nutrition*. Projects in India seek to meet the protein-energy and micronutrient needs of children and lactating women through supplements. In Niger the Bank is supporting the use of labor-saving devices to reduce energy expenditure, and in Malawi an effort is under way to increase food production and income generation in order to increase women's protein intake.

■ *Gynecological cancers*. Programs in Brazil, Chile, Ecuador, Romania, and Venezuela include detection and early treatment of cervical and breast cancer.

■ *Gender sensitivity in disease control*. In India the Bank has financed an innovative program to ensure gender sensitivity in disease-control efforts. The Leprosy Elimination Program provides training for female health and public education workers on the sociocultural factors that impede the identification and treatment of leprosy in women and on ways to promote self-care among women.

■ *Other sectors.* Bank projects also address the broader socioeconomic determinants of women's health. In Bangladesh and Burkina Faso, World Bank–assisted education projects include actions to improve female enrollment in schools. The Bank-financed Human Resource Development Project in Senegal includes a public education program for men and religious leaders aimed at countering negative attitudes toward family planning. In Ghana a Bank transport project provides supplemental food for women laborers.

Newer Bank projects focus more directly on women's health needs and are more comprehensive. For example, the Women's Health and Safe Motherhood Project being developed in the Philippines includes services related to maternal health, family planning, STDs, AIDS, and cervical cancer. The project provides support for NGOs working on women's health issues in the areas of communication, training, logistics, information systems, and partnerships with other agencies. Programs on such emerging issues as violence against women are also being developed.

Increasingly, population projects are adding reproductive health services to existing family planning programs. In Indonesia a new Bank-financed population project builds on the government's successful family planning program with the aim of broadening community-based health services to meet women's needs. The project includes training midwives to provide maternal health care at the village level, providing contraceptive information and services to adolescents, and educating the public on reproductive health and the role of women in society. This expansion represents a shift from the government's earlier strategy, which was more narrowly focused on increasing contraceptive acceptability and use and—since 1986—on promoting private sector provision of family planning services.

Partnership among Assistance Agencies

Substantial and lasting improvements in women's health will require a multisectoral approach. Assistance agencies should coordinate their inputs to maximize each agency's strengths and capabilities. Country programs could benefit from assistance agencies' comparative advantage in such areas as training, technical support, institutional development, and logistics management.

Within the United Nations system, WHO serves as the lead technical agency on health. WHO has prepared technical guidelines on many topics related to women's health, such as essential obstetric services and the Mother-Baby package (WHO forthcoming), and it is currently developing a counseling guide for healthy women. Many of the recommendations in this book are derived from

WHO's work. The United Nations Development Programme (UNDP) supports broad poverty reduction programs, the United Nations Children's Fund (UNICEF) addresses the problems of girls, and the United Nations Population Fund (UNFPA) provides family planning and related services. The World Bank, another member of the UN family, is the largest single provider of international financial assistance in the health sector. In addition, the Bank's strengths include its sectoral and economic analysis examining issues and appropriate strategies and its ability to engage in policy dialogue with core government ministries on resource allocation to support priority programs.

Bilateral agencies are also making important contributions to women's health. The Swedish International Development Authority (SIDA), which gives high priority to sexual and reproductive health, has collaborated with the World Bank and other assistance agencies in country programs. SIDA has developed a strategy on sexual and reproductive health that encourages governments to ensure the availability of essential reproductive health services. Several other bilateral assistance agencies have made reproductive health care a priority in their assistance programs.

International NGOs have national affiliates with close ties to the communities they serve, which often puts them in a good position to ensure that information is made available, controversial issues are addressed, and community needs are recognized. International NGOs can increase awareness, serve as a bridge between national organizations and international resources, stimulate debate and action, assist in the formulation of policy and development of programs, conduct research, and provide technical assistance. International organizations of health professionals such as physicians, nurses, and midwives can be helpful in establishing norms and standards for service delivery and disseminating information on effective approaches and new technologies.

Collaboration among assistance agencies has helped to advance women's health programs. For example, the Inter-Agency Group for Safe Motherhood supports safe motherhood programs. World Bank pilot projects in Bangladesh, Indonesia, and Zimbabwe have strengthened coordination among multilateral, bilateral, and nongovernmental organizations, improving the delivery of maternal health and family planning services. United Nations–sponsored international conferences on women, social development, and population provide a forum for discussing women's health policy and an opportunity for bringing concerns to the forefront of the development agenda and to the attention of a wide international audience.

An Agenda for Women's Health and Nutrition

International agencies can take six major steps to promote improvements in women's health and nutrition: persuade governments to give higher priority to women's health and nutrition; identify an institutional base for women's health and nutrition programs; promote greater use of gender-based data and pilot studies; support cost-effective women's health interventions; increase attention to changing health-related behaviors; and involve women in program planning and implementation.

Knowledge, policy support, and program development related to women's health problems vary greatly among countries. For example, strategies to address issues of new but increasing concern (such as gender violence, management of unsafe abortion, and STDs among adolescents) are relatively untested and could benefit from external assistance to support consciousness-raising, policy analysis, and pilot programs.

Influencing Policy Priorities

In many developing countries women's health and nutrition rank low among national priorities, even within the health sector. Assistance agencies can help make the case for greater attention to women's health on the basis of the multiple economic and social payoffs described in Chapter 1. Arguments to increase funding for women's health and nutrition programs should stress the far-reaching effects of a woman's poor health and the availability of cost-effective interventions.

Women represent a disproportionate share of the poor and so deserve particular consideration in programs to mitigate the potential adverse effects of structural and sectoral adjustment, particularly in the areas of nutrition and health. Related external assistance could take traditional forms, such as food-price subsidies and food distribution, or more innovative forms, such as social, health, nutrition, and education interventions designed to reach female children, adolescents, and adults.

Multilateral and multisectoral agencies such as the World Bank need to extend the policy dialogue beyond the ministry of health to include the ministries of finance, planning, education, and women's affairs, and to other sectors as appropriate. For most women's health issues, policy discussion should also include key decisionmakers and influential groups outside the government, such as health professionals, women's groups, and business leaders.

Creating an Institutional Base

International assistance agencies can designate an individual, department, or committee to take responsibility for women's health and nutrition programs and request that the ministries of health establish a similar institutional base. Such a base can give greater visibility to related programs, coordinate relevant activities, initiate or modify programs, and promote collaboration with other sectors. Because women's health and nutrition programs encompass a variety of service delivery modes and require collaboration with agencies outside the health sector, an institutional base can ensure program direction and coherence.

Encouraging Targeted Research

Without gender-disaggregated data, women's health problems can be easily overlooked. International agencies can support analyses that differentiate between males and females and can request that routine data reports include such differentiation. Disaggregation by age group is also important for program targeting.

Assistance agencies should support studies designed to broaden knowledge of women's health problems, encourage policy dialogue, improve the data base for project design and implementation, and mobilize resources in support of women's health.

In its sectoral work, the World Bank often compiles background material to support discussions on health policy and to assist governments in developing programs. In Brazil, for example, sectoral work documented the dimensions of women's health problems (including inadequate prenatal care, high rates of unsafe abortion, and unnecessarily high rates of cesarean section). In India and Uganda, sector analyses helped to identify women's health problems and constraints on women's use of health services.

Supporting Cost-Effective Services

Foreign assistance agencies can help governments match health services for women to each country's women's nutrition and health status profile. In most developing countries, assistance is needed to expand women's health and nutrition interventions on a national scale and to incorporate new components such as STD services and education on nutrition and safer sex.

Assistance agencies need to examine their own policies and program priorities in light of the cost-effective approaches identified in *World Development Report 1993* (World Bank 1993b). For example, few assistance agencies support abortion management, promotion of contraceptives to adolescents, and cervical cancer services. Missing the opportunity to include these services in assistance programs means high economic and social costs. In reorienting their women's health programs, assistance agencies should incorporate a life-cycle approach and give more emphasis to early prevention of disease and efforts to change behavior.

Promoting Behavioral Change

International assistance agencies can play a major role in influencing health agencies to give greater attention to preventive services and to become more involved in behavioral change interventions outside the traditional health care delivery system. Assistance agencies can facilitate links between health agencies and public and private institutions in other fields, provide funds and technical expertise for undertaking behavioral change interventions, and support mechanisms for exchanging information on effective strategies.

Increasing Women's Participation

Assistance agencies can do much more to involve women in health programs. Key areas for action include ensuring that in their own professional staffs women are adequately represented; including women on project planning, monitoring, and evaluation teams; encouraging health ministries to put more women in decisionmaking positions; involving women's organizations and female experts in all phases of program planning and implementation; incorporating mechanisms for soliciting women's feedback; and promoting the procurement of supplies and advisory services from female-owned businesses and women's cooperatives.

Assistance agencies can help to identify areas in which women's inputs would be useful and then facilitate their involvement. In addition, assistance agencies can insist that collaborating agencies publicize job vacancies, new contracts, and other opportunities so that women can compete for them. Links with women's groups, and particularly with women's income-generation projects, should be explored. For example, women's groups could create clinic signs, banners, badges, and other promotional materials.

Regional Problems and Priorities

Although women throughout the developing the world share common health problems, the key concerns vary from region to region. So, too, do the priorities for action.

Sub-Saharan Africa

Sub-Saharan Africa has the world's highest fertility and maternal mortality rates. Maternal health problems are exacerbated by poor prenatal and delivery care and by unsafe abortion, which accounts for 20 to 40 percent of all maternal mortality in the region. African countries also have some of the highest adolescent pregnancy rates in the world. By age 18 more than 40 percent of females in Côte d'Ivoire, Mali, and Senegal have already given birth (Population Reference Bureau 1992).

STDs and HIV/AIDS are a major cause of disability and death among African women and account for more than half the STD burden among women in developing countries. Infertility and cervical cancer, often caused by STDs, are common in some countries. Female genital mutilation is practiced in several countries of the region.

Priorities for improving women's health in Africa include increasing access to maternity care, family planning, safe services for abortion management, and STD services, and preventing genital mutilation, HIV infection, and violence against women. To deliver the necessary clinical and preventive services—and especially to extend services to rural areas—many countries will need to strengthen their health care infrastructure. Special initiatives for adolescents are needed because of the large numbers of young females at risk and the great potential for improving health through the postponement of sexual activity and childbearing, safer sex practices, and good nutrition.

South Asia

Throughout most of South Asia, women of all ages suffer the effects of gender discrimination. Discrimination and neglect are estimated to cause one in six deaths of female infants in Bangladesh, India, and Pakistan. In some areas gender-specific abuse is common, including sex selection through abortion, female infanticide, and injury and death associated with wife abuse and dowry demands. Other forms of discrimination, such as giving less food to female household members, restricting their access to health services, and imposing more physical work on girls and women, are also common. Women's lower status is also evident in lower school enrollment and retention rates.

Many women lack access to health care, especially maternity care, contraceptives, and safe services for abortion management. South Asia has a higher proportion of growth stunting among girls and anemia among pregnant women than any other region. Only one in three women receives prenatal care or has a trained attendant at delivery. Consequently, rates of death and disability associated with pregnancy and childbirth are high. STDs are widespread, and HIV infection is on the rise.

The key component of an agenda for women's health in South Asia is for health care providers to combat the effects of discrimination by expanding access to health services through such measures as training female health providers, conducting community education and outreach programs, and publicizing the importance of protecting female health. Expanding and improving the quality of women's health services are also important. Health programs need to give greater attention to the nutritional status of young girls and adolescents, as well as to detection and prompt referral of pregnancy-related complications. Intersectoral initiatives are needed to address the problems of early marriage and violence against women.

East and Southeast Asia

In certain countries, such as Laos and Cambodia, women's health conditions resemble those in South Asia or Africa. In other parts of East and Southeast Asia, women are attaining levels of health, education, and social status typical of middle-income countries. In East Asia 95 percent of women benefit from trained assistance during delivery, although less than half of all deliveries take place in institutions. There are considerable regional and urban-rural differences, however, reflecting the influence of lifestyle and economic status on disease patterns. For rural women, infectious diseases are a major cause of death, while urban women have higher rates of cardiovascular and cerebrovascular diseases and cervical and breast cancer. East Asia has the highest incidence of cervical cancer among the developing regions.

Maternal morbidity and mortality rates remain high in several countries in the region because adequate maternity care is not widespread (WHO 1991a). Contraceptive prevalence is relatively high in Indonesia, the Republic of Korea, Malaysia, and Thailand, but in some countries, such as the Philippines, a full range of contraceptive methods is not available. HIV/AIDS is growing more rapidly in Southeast Asia than in any other part of the world (USAID 1991). Increasingly, girls in their early teens are entering prostitution, often because of economic hardship or force.

Smoking and alcohol abuse among women are growing concerns in some parts of East Asia, as multinational tobacco firms increasingly target advertising to women. Women's health status is also influenced by discriminatory practices, such as sex selection in China and the Republic of Korea and female genital mutilation in parts of Indonesia and Malaysia.

Priorities for women's health services are likely to vary considerably within the region, depending on the existing health infrastructure and policies. In countries with limited services, health agencies will need to concentrate on expansion and improvement to ensure access to maternity care, family planning, and safe abortion services. Most countries in the region need to give additional attention to early prevention of disease among young and adolescent girls, especially by stressing the dangers of unprotected sex, tobacco use, and substance abuse. Where resources permit, cancer screening and treatment should be provided.

The Middle East and North Africa

Fertility rates in the Middle East and North Africa are among the highest in the world, almost equal to those of Sub-Saharan Africa. High fertility and early childbearing contribute to poor health among women. Contraceptive prevalence rates are low, and access to health care is poor. Cultural norms prevent many women from using existing health services. Female genital mutilation is practiced in some areas. Women's low status and low literacy levels, as well as lack of information and data on women's health issues, are major obstacles to improving female health.

The main priority in the region is to increase women's access to health care by better meeting their needs for female health care providers, convenient locations, and information on healthy behavior. Better maternity care is another pressing need in most countries. Women could also benefit substantially from improved access to contraception and a broader choice of methods.

Latin America and the Caribbean

In many Latin American countries, noncommunicable diseases cause more deaths and disability to women than communicable diseases and maternal and perinatal causes combined. Nevertheless, maternal mortality ratios in the region are higher than in other areas with comparable income levels, due in large part to unsafe abortion. Fertility is moderately high in most countries. Services are often inefficient and of poor quality. Tertiary and higher-level health facilities are overutilized for maternity care, and some countries have abnormally high rates of cesarean section deliveries, which adds to women's health risks.

Unwanted pregnancy, particularly among adolescents, is a serious problem. Although abortion is illegal in most countries in the region, abortion rates in some areas are among the world's highest. STDs are also a growing concern. Although the AIDS epidemic is in the early stages, the number of cases among women is projected to rise sharply by the year 2000 (PAHO 1993). Violence against women is increasingly recognized as a source of poor mental and physical health.

As the proportion of older people rises, problems such as cardiovascular and cerebrovascular diseases are becoming more significant among women. Breast cancer is increasingly common, particularly in the higher-income countries. Cervical cancer is also on the rise. Women's risk of disease is raised by such factors as high rates of smoking, obesity, and anemia; almost one in three women in the region is anemic (PAHO 1993).

The agenda for improving women's health in Latin America includes ensuring that low-income women have access to health care services, especially maternity care and family planning; developing strategies to meet the reproductive and sexual health needs of adolescents; addressing the problems of unwanted pregnancy and unsafe abortion; and promoting healthy behaviors, such as good nutrition, safer sex practices, and avoidance of smoking and obesity. Some countries will need to give more attention to specific problem areas such as overuse of tertiary health care facilities, unnecessary medical procedures, HIV/AIDS, violence against women, and inadequate assistance to women beyond reproductive age, including management of cervical and breast cancers.

Eastern Europe and Central Asia

Women's health status in Eastern Europe and Central Asia is lower than might be expected, given high levels of female education and a reasonably well developed health infrastructure. Shortages of drugs and supplies are common, as are outdated health care practices that are not always cost-effective. Although almost all women receive prenatal care, excessive emphasis is placed on diagnostic tests and not enough on counseling and prevention. Abortion, which is legal in many countries in the region, is the most common method of fertility regulation because contraceptives are largely unavailable; in fact, there are more abortions than live births. The needs of divorced, widowed, and elderly women require greater attention. In several countries women's health status is worsening, and their access to such services as legal, state-subsidized abortions is being threatened.

Key initiatives in a women's health agenda for the region include making family planning information and services more widely available to reduce reliance on abortion, providing more training to improve clinical practice, ensuring that adequate drugs and supplies are available, increasing the emphasis on preventive health care (particularly avoidance of tobacco, the value of exercise, and good nutrition), and addressing the needs of women beyond reproductive age.

Moving Forward

The task ahead is to apply what we know about women's health needs to concrete actions. We know that many women's health problems could be prevented or mitigated through low-cost interventions. We know that these interventions can work in low-income settings. We know that investments in women's health have multiple payoffs for the national economy, the community, individual families, and the next generation. What remains to be done is to pierce the veil of indifference and inertia that inhibits women's health and nutrition programs. Given a mandate for change, agencies and individuals can advance new initiatives and support more effective allocation of existing resources. For the countless millions of women struggling to meet their families' daily needs and make a better life for themselves and their children, such changes cannot come too soon.

Appendix

MAJOR HEALTH PROBLEMS AMONG FEMALES IN DEVELOPING COUNTRIES AND COST-EFFECTIVE INTERVENTIONS, 1990

Age group/ main causes of disease	Total DALYs lost from all diseases (millions)	Percentage of total disease burden for each age group[a]	Cost-effectiveness of existing interventions[b]	Cost of intervention per DALY saved
Ages 0–4	250			
Respiratory infections		18.5	High	$20–50
Perinatal causes		17.2	High	—
Diarrheal disease		16.2	High	$10–170
Childhood cluster[c]		10.7	High	$10–25
Congenital problems		6.5	Unassessed	—
Malaria		4.7	High	—
Protein-energy malnutrition		2.4	High	$63
Vitamin A deficiency		2.3	High	$1–4
Iodine deficiency		1.3	High	$8–37
Falls		1.2	Unassessed	—
Ages 5–14	67			
Intestinal helminths		12.3	High	$15–30
Childhood cluster[c]		8.6	High	$10–25
Respiratory infections		7.9	High	—
Diarrheal disease		7.1	High	—
Tuberculosis		5.7	High	$3–5
Malaria		4.9	High	$5–250
Motor vehicle injuries		3.7	Unassessed	—
Anemias		3.0	High	—
Epilepsy		2.6	Unassessed	—
STDs and HIV		2.4	High	$3–5

(Table continues on the following page.)

Age group/ main causes of disease	Total DALYs lost from all diseases (millions)	Percentage of total disease burden for each age group[a]	Cost-effectiveness of existing interventions[b]	Cost of intervention per DALY saved
Ages 15–44	155			
Maternal causes		18.0	High	$60–110
STDs		8.9	High	$10–15
Tuberculosis		7.0	High	$3–5
HIV		6.6	High	$3–5
Depressive disorders		5.8	Moderate	—
Self-inflicted injuries		3.2	Unassessed	—
Anemia		2.5	High	$4–13
Respiratory infections		2.5	High	—
Osteoarthritis		2.2	Unassessed	—
Motor vehicle injuries		2.1	Moderate	—
Ages 45–59	49			
Cerebrovascular diseases		8.7	Low	—
Tuberculosis		5.6	High	$3–5
Ischemic heart disease		4.7	Moderate	—
Peri-, endo- and myocarditis		3.2	Unassessed	—
Cataracts		3.1	High	$20–40
Periodontal disease		3.1	Unassessed	—
Chronic obstructive pulmonary diseases		2.8	Moderate	—
Diabetes mellitus		2.8	Moderate	—
Osteoarthritis		2.7	Unassessed	—
Cancer of the cervix		2.6	High	$150–200
Ages 60+	60			
Cerebrovascular diseases		16.5	Low	—
Ischemic heart disease		11.6	Moderate	—
Chronic obstructive pulmonary diseases		8.1	Moderate	—
Alzheimer's disease and other dementias		4.8	Unassessed	—
Respiratory infections		4.6	High	—
Peri-, endo- and myocarditis		3.6	Unassessed	—
Diabetes mellitus		2.4	Moderate	—
Tuberculosis		1.9	High	$3–5
Falls		1.8	Unassessed	—
Cataracts		1.6	High	—

a. Percentages do not total 100% because only the ten main causes of disease for each age group are listed.
b. Interventions of high cost-effectiveness are those that can be implemented for less than $100 per disability-adjusted life year (DALY) saved; those of moderate cost-effectiveness cost between $250 and $999 per DALY saved; and those of low cost-effectiveness cost more than $1,000 per DALY saved. (Few interventions are in the range of $100 to $250 per DALY saved.) "Unassessed" indicates diseases for which preventive and therapeutic interventions have not been evaluated in terms of cost-effectiveness.
c. Vaccine-preventable diseases of childhood.
Source: World Bank 1993b.

Bibliography

Acsadi, George T. F., and Gwendolyn Johnson-Acsadi. 1993. "Socio-economic, Cultural, and Legal Factors Affecting Girls' and Women's Health." Women's Health and Nutrition Work Program Working Paper Series. World Bank, Population, Health and Nutrition Department, Washington, D.C.

Adebajo, Christine, Carol Kazi, Elisabeth Crane, and Ian Todreas. 1990. "Community Mobilization: Steps Toward Eradicating Female Circumcision and Other Harmful Traditional Practices in Nigeria." Paper presented at the 118th Annual Meeting of the American Public Health Association, New York, September 30–October 4.

Ajayi, Ayo A., Leah T. Marangu, Janice Miller, and John M. Paxman. 1991. "Adolescent Sexuality and Fertility in Kenya: A Survey of Knowledge, Perceptions and Practices." *Studies in Family Planning* 22(4):205–16.

Ainsworth, Martha, and Mead Over. 1994. "AIDS in African Development." *Research Observer* 9(2):203–40.

APWRCN (Asian and Pacific Women's Resource Collection Network). 1989. *Health.* Asian and Pacific Women's Resource and Action Series. Kuala Lumpur, Malaysia: Asian and Pacific Development Centre.

Behrman, Jere R. 1990. *The Action of Human Resources and Poverty on One Another: What We Have Yet to Learn.* LSMS Working Paper 74. Washington, D.C.: World Bank.

Bledsoe, Caroline H., and Barney Cohen, eds. 1993. *Social Dynamics of Adolescent Fertility in Sub-Saharan Africa.* Washington, D.C.: National Academy Press.

Brennan, Maureen. 1992. "Training Traditional Birth Attendants." *Postgraduate Doctor Africa* 11(1):16.

Bruce, Judith. 1990. "Fundamental Elements of Quality of Care: A Simple Framework." *Studies in Family Planning* 22(November–December):343–47.

CDC (Centers for Disease Control). 1991. *1987 Guatemala Demographic and Health Survey: Further Analysis of Data.* Vol. B, *Young Adult Module.* Atlanta, Ga.

———. 1994. *Morbidity and Mortality Weekly Report* 43(16).

Chalmers, Ian, Murray Enkin, and Marc Kierse. 1989. *Effective Care in Pregnancy and Childbirth.* New York: Oxford University Press.

Chatterjee, Meera. 1991. *Indian Women: Their Health and Productivity.* Discussion Paper 109. Washington, D.C.: World Bank.

Chatterjee, Meera, and Julian Lambert. 1989. "Women and Nutrition: Reflections from India and Pakistan." *Food and Nutrition Bulletin* 11(4):13–28.

Church, Cathleen A., and Judith Geller. 1989. "Lights! Camera! Action! Promoting Family Planning with TV, Video, and Film." *Population Reports* (Johns Hopkins University) Series J, No. 28 (December).

CIAES (Centro de Investigación, Asesoria, y Educación en Salud). 1991. "Qualitative Research on Knowledge, Attitudes and Practices Related to Women's Reproductive Health." Working Paper 9. MotherCare, Arlington, Va.

Coale, Ansley J., and Paul G. Demeny. 1983. *Regional Model Life Tables and Stable Populations.* 2nd ed. New York: Academic Press.

Coeytaux, Francine. 1989. *Celebrating Mother and Child on the Fortieth Day: The Sfax, Tunisia Postpartum Program.* Quality/Calidad/Qualité Series, No. 1. New York: Population Council.

Das Gupta, Monica. 1987. "Selective Discrimination against Female Children in Rural Punjab, India." *Population and Development Review* 13:1(March):77–100.

DeMaeyer, E. M., and M. Adiels-Tegman. 1985. "The Prevalence of Anemia in the World." *World Health Statistics Quarterly* 38(3):302–16.

Dixon-Mueller, Ruth. 1990. "Abortion Policy and Women's Health in Developing Countries." *International Journal of Health Services* 20:297–314.

Edgerton, V. R., G. W Gardner, Y. Ohira, K. A. Gunarwardena, and B. Senewiratne. 1979. "Iron-Deficiency Anaemia and Its Effect on Worker Productivity and Activity Patterns." *British Medical Journal* 2:1546–49.

Ekwempu, C. C., D. Maine, M. B. Olorukoba, B. Essien, and M. N. Kisseka. 1990. "Structural Adjustment and Health in Africa." Letter. *Lancet* (July 7):56–57.

Ettling, M. B., K. Thimasarn, S. Krachaiklin, and P. Bualombai. 1989. "Evaluation of Malaria Clinics in Maesot, Thailand: Use of Serology to Assess Coverage." *Transactions of the Royal Society of Tropical Medicine and Hygiene.* 83:325–30.

Fauveau, Vincent. 1991. "Matlab Maternity Care Program." Review paper prepared for the World Bank Department of Population and Human Resources, Washington, D.C.

Favin, Michael N., and M. Griffiths. 1991. "Social Marketing of Micronutrients in Developing Countries." Manoff Group, Inc., Washington, D.C.

FHI (Family Health International). 1992. "Cameroon Launches Social Marketing of Antibiotics." *Network* 12(4):14–15.

Figueroa, Blanca. 1992. "Adding Color to Life: Illustrated Health Materials for Women in Peru." In *By and For Women: Involving Women in the Development of Reproductive Health Care Materials.* Quality/Calidad/Qualité Series, No. 4. New York: Population Council.

Fishman, Claudia, D. Touré, and Peter Gottert. 1991. "Nutrition Promotion in Mali: Highlights from a Rural Integrated Nutrition Communication Program." Paper presented at the 6th International Conference of International Nutrition Planners Forum, Paris, September 4–6. Academy for Educational Development, Washington, D.C.

Freedman, Ronald, and Bernard Berelson. 1976. "The Record of Family Planning Programs." *Studies in Family Planning* 7(11):3–40.

Freedman, Ronald, and Ann Klimas Blanc. 1991. "Fertility Transition: An Update."
In *Proceedings of the Demographic and Health Surveys World Conference,* Vol.
1. Columbia, Md.: Institute for Resource Development/Macro International.

Gallen, Moira E., Laurie Liskin, and Neeraj Kak. 1986. "Men—New Focus for Family
Planning Programs." *Population Reports* (Johns Hopkins University) Series J,
No. 33 (November–December).

Gay, Jill. 1993. "Women's Access to Quality Health Services and Empowerment to
Promote their Own Health." Women's Health and Nutrition Work Program Work-
ing Paper Series. World Bank, Department of Population, Health and Nutrition,
Washington, D.C.

Georgetown University School of Medicine. 1990. *Guidelines for Breastfeeding in
Family Planning and Child Survival Programs.* Washington, D.C.: Georgetown
University/Institute for International Studies in Natural Family Planning.

Gertler, Paul, and Jacques van der Gaag. 1990. *The Willingness to Pay for Medical
Care: Evidence from Two Developing Countries.* Baltimore: Johns Hopkins University Press.

Ghassemi, Hossein. 1990. "Women, Food and Nutrition: Issues in Need of a Global
Focus." In UN ACC/SCN, *Women and Nutrition.* UN ACC/SCN Symposium Report,
Nutrition Policy Discussion Paper 6:145–65. Geneva: United Nations Adminis-
trative Committee on Coordination/Subcommittee on Nutrition.

Green, Cynthia P. 1989. *Media Promotion of Breastfeeding: A Decade's Experience.*
Washington, D.C.: Academy for Educational Development.

Grunseit, A., and S. Kippax. 1993. *Effects of Sex Education on Young People's Sexual
Behavior.* Geneva: World Health Organization.

Harrison, K. A., A. F. Fleming, N. D. Briggs, and C. E. Rossiter. 1985. "Growth
During Pregnancy in Nigerian Teenage Primigravidae." *British Journal of Ob-
stetrics and Gynecology* 5(Supplement):32–39.

Heise, Lori. 1993. "Violence Against Women: The Missing Agenda." In Marjorie A.
Koblinsky, Judith Timyan, and Jill Gay, eds., *The Health of Women: A Global
Perspective.* Boulder, Colo.: Westview Press.

Heise, Lori L., Jacqueline Pitanguy, and Adrienne Germain. 1994. *Violence Against
Women: The Hidden Health Burden.* Discussion Paper 255. Washington, D.C.:
World Bank.

Henshaw, Stanley K. 1990. "Induced Abortion: A World Review, 1990." *Family Planning Perspectives* 22:76–89.

Herz, Barbara, and Anthony R. Measham. 1987. *The Safe Motherhood Initiative: Proposals for Action.* Discussion Paper 9. Washington, D.C.: World Bank.

Herz, Barbara, Kalanidhi Subbarao, Masoma Habid, and Laura Raney. 1991. *Letting
Girls Learn: Promising Approaches in Primary and Secondary Education.* Discussion Paper 133. Washington, D.C.: World Bank.

Hira, S. K., G. J. Bhat, D. M. Chikamata, B. Nkowane, G. Tembo, P. L. Perine, and A.
Meheus. 1990. "Syphilis Intervention in Pregnancy: Zambian Demonstration
Project." *Genitourinary Medicine* 66:159–64.

Hovell, M. F., and others. 1988. "Occupational Health Risks for Mexican Women: The
Case of the Maquiladora along the Mexican–United States Border." *International Journal of Health Services* 18(4):617–27.

IAC (Inter-African Committee on Traditional Practices Affecting the Health of Women and Children). 1993. "Profile of a National Committee: Burkina Faso." *IAC Newsletter* 15(December):13.

Ibrahim, Barbara, and Nadia Farah. 1992. "Women's Lives and Health: The Cairo Women's Health Book Collective." In *By and For Women: Involving Women in the Development of Reproductive Health Care Materials.* Quality/Calidad/Qualité Series, No. 4. New York: Population Council.

ICRW (International Center for Research on Women). 1989. *Strengthening Women: Health Research Priorities for Women in Developing Countries.* Washington, D.C.

IPPF (International Planned Parenthood Federation). 1992. "Adolescent Prostitutes in Thailand." *Open File* (February):9.

———. 1993. "Sexual Health Program: Program Description." Internal document. London.

Jamison, Dean T. 1993. "Disease Control Priorities in Developing Countries: An Overview." In Dean T. Jamison, W. Henry Mosley, Anthony R. Measham, and José Luis Bobadilla, eds., *Disease Control Priorities in Developing Countries.* New York: Oxford University Press.

Jamison, Dean T., W. Henry Mosley, Anthony R. Measham, and José Luis Bobadilla, eds. 1993. *Disease Control Priorities in Developing Countries.* New York: Oxford University Press.

Johnson, Brooke R., Janie Benson, and Beth Leibson Hawkins. 1992. "Reducing Resource and Reducing Quality of Care with MVA." *IPAS Advances in Abortion Care* (Carrboro, N.C.) 2(2):1–5.

Kay, Bonnie J., Adrienne Germain, and Maggie Bangser. 1991. *The Bangladesh Women's Health Coalition.* Quality/Calidad/Qualité Series, No. 3. New York: Population Council.

Keyfitz, Nathan, and Wilhelm Flieger. 1990. *World Population Growth and Aging: Demographic Trends in the Late Twentieth Century.* Chicago: University of Chicago Press.

Khan, Atiqur Rahman, Farida Akter Jahan, and S. Firoza Begum. 1986. "Maternal Mortality in Rural Bangladesh: The Jamalpur District." *Studies in Family Planning* 17(1):7–12.

King, J., and others. 1986. *Programme Review of CARE MCH CD and SNP Title II Programme in India: Evaluation Report.* New Delhi: U.S. Agency for International Development.

Kizza, A. P., and K. O. Rogo. 1990. "Assessment of the Manual Vacuum Aspiration (MVA) Equipment in the Management of Incomplete Abortion." *East African Medical Journal* 67:812–22.

Krieger, Laurie, and Mohamed ElFeraly. 1991. "Male Doctor, Female Patient: Access to Health Care in Egypt." Paper presented at the Annual Meeting of the National Council for International Health, Washington, D.C., June 23–26.

Kutzin, Joseph. 1993a. "Cost-Effectiveness Issues in Women's Health." World Bank, Population, Health and Nutrition Department, Washington, D.C.

———. 1993b. "Obstacles to Women's Access: Issues and Options for More Effective Interventions to Improve Women's Health." HRO Working Paper 13. World

Bank, Human Resources Development and Operations Policy Department, Washington, D.C.

Kwast, Barbara. 1991. "Shortage of Midwives: The Effect on Family Planning." *IPPF Medical Bulletin* 25(3):1–3.

————. 1993. "Safe Motherhood—The First Decade." Paper presented at the 23rd International Congress of the International Confederation of Midwives, Vancouver, May 9–14.

Lande, Robert. 1993. "Controlling Sexually Transmitted Diseases." *Population Reports* (Johns Hopkins University) Series L, No. 9 (June).

Lande, Robert E., and Richard Blackburn. 1989. "Pharmacists and Family Planning." *Population Reports* (Johns Hopkins University) Series J, No. 37.

Leslie, Joanne. 1991. "Women's Nutrition: The Key to Improving Family Health in Developing Countries?" *Health Policy and Planning* 6(1):1–19.

————. 1992. "Women's Lives and Women's Health: Using Social Science Research to Promote Better Health for Women." *Journal of Woman's Health* 1(4):307–18.

Leslie, Joanne, and Geeta Rao Gupta. 1989. *Utilization of Formal Services for Maternal Nutrition and Health Care in the Third World.* Washington, D.C.: International Center for Research on Women.

Leslie, Joanne, Margaret Lycette, and Mayra Buvinic. 1988. "Weathering Economic Crises: The Crucial Role of Women in Health." In David E. Bell and Michael R. Reich, eds., *Health, Nutrition, and Economic Crises: Approaches to Policy in the Third World.* Dover, Mass.: Auburn House.

Li, Ruowei, Xuecun Chen, Huaicheng Yan, Paul Deurenberg, Lars Garby, and Joseph Hautvast. 1994. "Functional Consequences of Iron Supplementation in Iron-Deficient Female Cotton Mill Workers in Beijing, China." *American Journal of Clinical Nutrition* 59(4):908–13.

Lindsay, Robert. 1993. "Prevention and Treatment of Osteoporosis." *Lancet* 341(March 27):801–5.

Liskin, Laurie, Cathleen Church, Phyllis T. Piotrow, and John A. Harris. 1989. "AIDS Education—A Beginning." *Population Reports* (Johns Hopkins University) Series L, No. 8.

Litvack, Jenny I., and Claude Bodart. 1993. "User Fees Plus Quality Equals Improved Access to Health Care: Results of a Field Experiment in Cameroon." *Social Science and Medicine* 37(3):369–83.

Locay, Luis, Warren Sanderson, and Ethel Carillo Weeks. 1990. *Prenatal Care in Peru.* Washington, D.C.: International Center for Research on Women.

Lopez, Alan D. 1993. "Causes of Death in Industrial and Developing Countries: Estimates for 1985–90." In Dean T. Jamison, W. Henry Mosley, Anthony R. Measham, and José Luis Bobadilla, eds., *Disease Control Priorities in Developing Countries.* New York: Oxford University Press.

Marques, Magaly. 1993. *Gente Joven/Young People: A Dialogue on Sexuality with Adolescents in Mexico.* Quality/Calidad/Qualité Series, No. 5. New York: Population Council.

Matovina, Michael. 1992. "Female Genital Mutilation." Information sheet. World Bank, Africa Technical Department, Gender Team, Washington, D.C.

McLaurin, Katie E., Charlotte E. Hord, and Merrill Wolfe. 1991. "Health Systems' Role in Abortion Care: The Need for a Pro-active Approach." In *Issues in Abortion Care*, vol. 1. Carrboro, N.C.: International Projects Assistance Services.

Mensch, Barbara. 1993. "Quality of Care: A Neglected Dimension." In Marge Koblinsky, Judith Timyan, and Jill Gay, eds., *The Health of Women: A Global Perspective*. Boulder, Colo.: Westview Press.

Merchant, Kathleen. 1993. "New Directions in Policies to Improve the Nutritional Status of Women." Women's Health and Nutrition Work Program Working Paper Series. World Bank, Population, Health and Nutrition Department, Washington, D.C.

Miller, Anthony B. 1992. "Cervical Cancer Screening Programmes: Managerial Guidelines." Geneva: World Health Organization.

Miller, Anthony B., J. Chamberlain, N. E. Day, M. Hakama, and P. C. Prorok. 1990. "Report of a Workshop of the UICC Project on Evaluation of Screening for Cancer." *International Journal of Cancer* 46:761–69.

Moses, S., F. Manji, J. E. Bradley, N. J. D. Nagelkerke, M. A. Malisa, and F. A. Plummer. 1992. "Impact of User Fees on Attendance at a Referral Centre for Sexually Transmitted Diseases in Kenya." *Lancet* 340:463–66.

Moses, S., F. Plummer, E. Ngugi, N. Nagelkerke, A. Anzala, and J. Ndinya-Achola. 1991. "Controlling HIV in Africa: Effectiveness and Cost of an Intervention in a High-Frequency STD Transmitter Core Group." *AIDS* 5(4):407–11.

Mwabu, Germano, Martha Ainsworth, and Andrew Nyamete. 1993. "Quality of Medical Care and Choice of Medical Treatment in Kenya: An Empirical Analysis." Technical Working Paper 9. World Bank, Africa Technical Department, Human Resources and Poverty Division, Washington, D.C.

Nortman, Dorothy L., and Jorge Halvas. 1986. "A Cost-Benefit Analysis of the Mexican Social Security Administration's Family Planning Program." *Studies in Family Planning* 17(1):1–6.

Omran, Abdel R., and C. C. Standley. 1976. "Family Formation and Maternal Health." In *Family Formation Patterns and Health: An International Collaborative Study in India, Iran, Lebanon, Philippines, and Turkey*. Geneva: World Health Organization.

———. 1981. "Family Formation and Maternal Health." In *Further Studies on Family Formation Patterns and Health*. Geneva: World Health Organization.

Over, Mead, and Peter Piot. 1993. "HIV Infection and Sexually Transmitted Diseases." In Dean T. Jamison, W. Henry Mosley, Anthony R. Measham, and José Luis Bobadilla, eds., *Disease Control Priorities in Developing Countries*. New York: Oxford University Press.

PAHO (Pan-American Health Organization). 1993. *Gender, Women and Health in the Americas*. Scientific Publication No. 541. Washington D.C.: PAHO/WHO.

Paltiel, Freda L. 1993. "Women's Mental Health: A Global Perspective." In Marge Koblinsky, Judith Timyan, and Jill Gay, eds., *The Health of Women: A Global Perspective*. Boulder, Colo.: Westview Press.

Panos Institute. 1989. *AIDS and Children: A Family Disease*. London.

Parker, Laurie Noto, Geeta Rao Gupta, Kathleen Kurz, and Kathleen Merchant. 1990. *Better Health for Women: Research Results from the Maternal Nutrition and*

Health Care Program. Washington, D.C.: International Center for Research on Women.

Parkin, D. M., E. Laara, and C. S. Muir. 1988. "Estimates of the Worldwide Frequency of Sixteen Major Cancers in 1980." *International Journal of Cancer* 41(2):184–97.

PCS (Population Communication Services). 1992. *Media and Behavior Change.* Baltimore: Johns Hopkins University Press.

Pebley, Anne, and Sajeda Amin. 1991. "The Impact of a Public-Health Intervention on Sex Differentials in Childhood Mortality in Rural Punjab, India." *Health Transition Review* 1(2):143–69.

Piot, Peter, and Jane Rowley. 1992. "Economic Impact of Reproductive Tract Infections and Resources for Their Control." In Adrienne Germain, King K. Holmes, Peter Piot, and Judith N. Wasserheit, eds., *Reproductive Tract Infections: Global Impact and Priorities for Women's Reproductive Health.* New York: Plenum Press.

Poovan, Pamela, F. Kifle, and Barbara Kwast. 1990. "A Maternity Waiting Home Reduces Obstetric Catastrophes." *World Health Forum* 11:440–45.

Popular Education Research Group. 1992. *Women Educating to End Violence Against Women.* Toronto.

Population Reference Bureau. 1992. *Adolescent Women in Sub-Saharan Africa.* Washington, D.C.

Post, May Thein Hto. 1993. "Reproductive Tract Infections, HIV/AIDS and Women's Health." HRO Working Paper 15. World Bank, Human Resources Development and Operations Policy Department, Washington, D.C.

Ravindran, Sundari. 1986. "Health Implications of Sex Discrimination in Childhood." WHO/UNICEF/FHE 86.2. World Health Organization and UNICEF, Geneva.

Rogow, Debbie. 1990. *Man/Hombre/Homme: Meeting Male Reproductive Health Care Needs in Latin America.* Quality/Calidad/Qualité Series, No. 2. New York: Population Council.

Rojanapithayakorn, Wiwat. 1992. "100 Percent Condom Use Seeks to Slow HIV Spread." *Network* (Family Health International, Durham, N.C.) 13(May):4.

Rosenfield, Alan. 1989. "Maternal Mortality in Developing Countries: An Ongoing but Neglected 'Epidemic'." *Journal of the American Medical Association* 262:376–79.

Rosenhouse, Sandra. 1989. *Identifying the Poor: Is "Headship" a Useful Concept?* LSMS Working Paper 58. Washington D.C.: World Bank.

Ross, John A., W. Parker Mauldin, and Vincent C. Miller. 1993. *Family Planning and Population: A Compendium of International Statistics.* New York: Population Council.

Rovner, Sandy. 1993. "Many Toxins Target Women Specifically." *Washington Post Health Magazine* June 29:5.

Royston, Erica, and Sue Armstrong, eds. 1989. *Preventing Maternal Death.* Geneva: World Health Organization.

Sargent, Carolyn. 1989. *Maternity, Medicine and Power: Reproductive Decisions in Urban Benin.* Berkeley: University of California Press.

Schultz, T. Paul. 1989. "Returns to Women's Education." WPS 001. World Bank, Population and Human Resources Department, Washington, D.C.

Schulz, K. F., J. M. Schulte, and S. M. Berman. 1992. "Maternal Health and Child Survival: Opportunities to Protect Both Women and Children from the Adverse Consequences of Reproductive Tract Infections." In Adrienne Germain, King K. Holmes, Peter Piot, and Judith N. Wasserheit, eds., *Reproductive Tract Infections: Global Impact and Priorities for Women's Reproductive Health.* New York: Plenum Press.

Senderowitz, Judith. Forthcoming. *Reassessing the Passage to Adulthood: Issues and Strategies for Adolescents' Health.* Discussion Paper. Washington, D.C.: World Bank.

Servicio Nacional de la Mujer. 1991. *Perfil de la Mujer: Argumentos Para un Cambio.* Santiago, Chile.

Sherris, Jacqueline D., and G. Fox. 1983. "Infertility and Sexually Transmitted Diseases: A Public Health Challenge." *Population Reports* (Johns Hopkins University) Series L, No. 4.

Sherris, Jacqueline D., Elisa S. Wells, Vivien Davis Tsu, and Amie Bishop. 1993. "Cervical Cancer in Developing Countries: A Situation Analysis." Women's Health and Nutrition Work Program Working Paper Series. World Bank, Population, Health and Nutrition Department, Washington, D.C.

Simmons, Ruth, Michael Koenig, and Zahidul Huque. 1990. "Maternal-Child Health and Family Planning: User Perspectives and Service Constraints in Rural Bangladesh." *Studies in Family Planning* 21(4):187–96.

Stansfield, Sally K., Gordon S. Smith, and William P. McGreevey. 1993. "Injury." In Dean T. Jamison, W. Henry Mosley, Anthony R. Measham, and José Luis Bobadilla, eds., *Disease Control Priorities in Developing Countries.* New York: Oxford University Press.

Steketee, Richard. 1989. "Recent Findings in Perinatal Malaria." Working paper for the 19th International Congress of Pediatrics, Paris, July 23–28.

Strauss, John, Paul Gertler, Omar Rahman, and Kristin Fox. 1992. *Gender and Life-Cycle Differentials in the Patterns and Determinants of Adult Health.* Santa Monica, Calif.: Rand Corporation and Ministry of Health, Government of Jamaica.

Strong, Michael A. 1992. "The Health of Adults in the Developing World: The View from Bangladesh." *Health Transition Review* 2(2):215–24.

Sundström, Kajsa. 1993. "Abortion: A Reproductive Health Issue." World Bank Women's Health and Nutrition Work Program Working Paper Series. World Bank, Population, Health and Nutrition Department, Washington, D.C.

Thaddeus, Sereen, and Deborah Maine. 1990. *Too Far to Walk: Maternal Mortality in Context.* New York: Center for Population and Family Health, School of Public Health, Faculty of Medicine, Columbia University.

Tinker, Anne, Patricia Daly, Cynthia Green, Helen Saxenian, Rama Lakshminarayanan, and Kirrin Gill. 1994. *Women's Health and Nutrition: Making a Difference.* Discussion Paper 256. Washington, D.C.: World Bank.

Tinker, Anne, and Marjorie A. Koblinsky, with Patricia Daly, Cleone Rooney, Charlotte Leighton, Marcia Griffiths, A. A. Zahidul Huque, and Barbara Kwast. 1993. *Making Motherhood Safe.* Discussion Paper 202. Washington, D.C.: World Bank.

Toubia, Nahid. 1993. *Female Genital Mutilation: A Call for Global Action.* New York: Women, Ink.

Tout, Ken 1989. *Aging in Developing Countries.* New York: Oxford University Press.

UN (United Nations), Department of International Economic and Social Affairs. 1991. *The World's Women 1970–1990: Trends and Statistics.* New York.

———. 1993. *World Population Prospects: The 1992 Revision.* ST/ESA/SER.A/135. New York.

UN ACC/SCN (United Nations Administrative Committee on Coordination/Subcommittee on Nutrition). 1992. *Second Report on the World Nutrition Situation.* Vol. 1, *Global and Regional Results.* Geneva.

UNDP (United Nations Development Program). 1993. *Young Women: Silence, Susceptibility and the HIV Epidemic.* New York: UNDP HIV and Development Program.

USAID (United States Agency for International Development). 1991. *HIV Infection and AIDS: A Report to Congress on the USAID Program for Prevention and Control of HIV Infection.* Washington, D.C..

Van Look, Paul F. A. 1990. "Postcoital Contraception." *Outlook* 8(3):2–6.

Villar, J., and J. Rivera. 1988. "Nutritional Supplementation during Two Consecutive Pregnancies and the Interim Lactation Period: Effect on Birth Weight." *Pediatrics* 81(1):51–57.

Vlassof, Carol, and Elssy Bonilla. 1992. "Gender Differences in the Determinants and Consequences of Tropical Diseases: What Do We Know?" World Health Organization, Special Programme for Research and Training in Tropical Diseases, Geneva.

Walley, John, Bekele Tefera, and Mary Anne McDonald. 1991. "Integrating Health Services: The Experience of NGOs in Ethiopia." *Health Policy and Planning* 6(4):327–35.

Weinstein, Judith, Elizabeth Oliveras, and Noel MacIntosh. 1993. "Women's Reproductive Health in the Central Asian Republics." World Bank, Population, Health and Nutrition Department, Washington, D.C.

Westoff, Charles F., and Luis Hernando Ochoa. 1991. "Unmet Need and the Demand for Family Planning." *DHS Comparative Studies* No. 5. Columbia, Md.: Macro Systems/Institute for Resource Development.

White, S. M., R. G. Thorpe, and Deborah Maine. 1987. "Emergency Obstetric Surgery Performed by Nurses in Zaire." *Lancet* 2:612–13.

WHO (World Health Organization). 1986. *Young People's Health: A Challenge for Society.* Geneva.

———. 1989. "Youth and Reproductive Health." *The Health of Youth: Facts for Action.* No. 6. Geneva.

———. 1991a. *Maternal Mortality: A Global Fact Book.* Geneva.

———. 1991b. "Trained Women Health Providers: Their Types, Number and Deployment in Developing Countries." Internal document. Geneva.

———. 1992a. *Approaches to Adolescent Health and Development: A Compendium of Projects and Programmes.* Geneva.

———. 1992b. *Global Programme on AIDS: 1991 Progress Report.* Geneva.

————. 1992c. *Women's Health: Across Age and Frontier*. Geneva.

————. 1993a. *Coverage of Maternity Care: A Tabulation of Available Information*. WHO/FHE/MSM/93.7 Geneva: WHO Division of Family Health.

————. 1993b. *Global Health News and Review*. 1(2).

————. 1993c. "13 Million HIV Positive Women by 2000." Press release. WHO/69, September 7. Geneva.

————. Forthcoming. *Mother and Baby Package*. Geneva: WHO Maternal Health and Safe Motherhood Program.

WHO (World Health Organization) and UNICEF (United Nations Children's Fund). 1992. *Low Birth Weight: A Tabulation of Available Information*. WHO/MCH/92.2. Geneva: WHO Maternal Health and Safe Motherhood Programme.

Winikoff, Beverly, Charles Carignan, Elizabeth Bernardik, and Patricia Semeraro. 1991. "Medical Services to Save Mothers' Lives: Feasible Approaches to Reducing Maternal Mortality." Working Paper 4. Population Council, New York.

World Bank. 1992. *World Development Report 1992: Development and the Environment*. New York: Oxford University Press.

————. 1993a. *Effective Family Planning Programs*. Washington, D.C.

————. 1993b. *World Development Report 1993: Investing in Health*. New York: Oxford University Press.

————. 1994. *Enhancing Women's Participation in Economic Development*. A World Bank Policy Paper. Washington, D.C.

————. Forthcoming. *Enriching Lives: Overcoming Vitamin and Mineral Malnutrition in Developing Countries*. Washington, D.C.

Yinger, Nancy, Population Reference Bureau, Demographic and Health Surveys Project of Macro International, and the Division of Reproductive Health of the Centers for Disease Control. 1992. *Adolescent Sexual Activity and Childbearing in Latin America and the Caribbean: Risks and Consequences*. Washington, D.C.: International Programs, Population Reference Bureau.

Young, Mary Eming. 1993. "Women's Health Beyond Reproductive Age: The Picture in Developing Countries." World Bank Women's Health and Nutrition Work Program Working Paper Series. World Bank, Population, Health and Nutrition Department, Washington, D.C.

Younis, N. H., H. Zurayk Khattab, and others. 1993. "A Community Study of Gynecological and Related Morbidities in Rural Egypt." *Studies in Family Planning* 24(3).

Zewdie, Debrework. 1993. "Men, Women and AIDS." Paper presented at the 13th International Conference on AIDS in Africa, Marrakech, December 12–16. AIDS Control and Prevention Project, Arlington, Va.